ST. PETERSBURG'S HISTORIC
African American Neighborhoods

St. Petersburg's Historic
African American
Neighborhoods

Rosalie Peck & Jon Wilson

THE
History
PRESS

Published by The History Press
Charleston, SC 29403
www.historypress.net

First published 2008

ISBN 9781540229151

Library of Congress Cataloging-in-Publication Data

Wilson, Jon, 1945-
St. Petersburg's historic African American neighborhoods : community, culture, and
connection / Jon Wilson and Rosalie Peck.
p. cm.
Includes bibliographical references.
ISBN-13: 9781540229151
1. African American neighborhoods--Florida--Saint Petersburg--History. 2.
African Americans--Florida--Saint Petersburg--History. 3. Historic sites--Florida-
-Saint Petersburg. 4. African Americans--Florida--Saint Petersburg--Biography. 5.
Community life--Florida--Saint Petersburg--History. 6. African Americans--Florida--
Saint Petersburg--Social life and customs. 7. Saint Petersburg (Fla.)--History. 8. Saint
Petersburg (Fla.)--Social life and customs. 9. Saint Petersburg (Fla.)--Biography. 10. Oral
history--Florida--Saint Petersburg. I. Peck, Rosalie. II. Title.
F319.S24W55 2008
975.9'63--dc22
2007045272

Contents

Acknowledgements

Referring to a widely known presidential candidate named Clinton, retired police officer James King said, "Hillary was right. It takes a village to bring up a child." Quoted in this book, King was talking about the way a community pitched in to rear youngsters back in the day.

Well, it takes a community to produce a book, too.

We would like to thank the staff of *The Weekly Challenger*, and particularly Ethel Johnson, the newspaper's Publisher/CEO, and Dianne Speights, the general/advertising manager. Their work inspired us, and many of the newspaper's archival images help to illustrate this book.

Likewise, several editors at the *St. Petersburg Times* have provided encouragement during various stages of writing history. Among them are Neil Brown, Stephen Buckley, Jim Verhulst and Sandra Gadsden. These newsroom leaders emphasized coverage of St. Petersburg's African American neighborhoods, and many of the story lines have found their way into this book.

The work of ace reporters Anne Lindberg, Waveney Ann Moore and Donna Winchester guided us toward important pieces of recent history.

Chief *Times* librarian Tim Rozgonyi and researcher Mary Mellstrom granted access to old files and other research materials.

Artist Don Morris provided an illustration important to understanding the historic neighborhoods.

Thanks go to Lee Handford of The History Press, who graciously fielded numerous questions as deadlines approached, and to her colleague Jaime Muehl, who edited the manuscript and made it better.

Sometimes people contribute without knowing they have done so, and such is the case with Evelyn Newman Phillips and Scott Taylor Hartzell. Newman is a scholar who did groundbreaking work on St. Petersburg's African American neighborhoods for her doctoral dissertation. Hartzell is among St. Petersburg's more prolific, ambitious and interesting historians. The work of both these individuals is cited in this book.

We offer particular thanks to professors Raymond Arsenault and Gary Mormino at the University of South Florida, St. Petersburg. Co-directors of the university's Florida Studies Department, they are mentors who offer inspiration and depths of knowledge that they have been happy to share. Mormino is a consummate microfilm detective who rarely appears without a sheaf of useful old newspaper articles in hand.

Thanks also go to Ray Sanderlin for encouraging a line of inquiry about the "courageous twelve" police officers who fought for the right to fully represent their profession.

Goliath Davis III, PhD, a St. Petersburg deputy mayor, opened numerous doors. The city's Linda Kinsey helped with archival images.

Norman Jones II, who has made African American history both his vocation and avocation, provided rare documents and photographs.

Dozens of people shared their affection for their communities, in terms of both individual neighborhoods and the wider city. In one way or another, they helped keep the authors' work moving forward. We would like to thank C. Patricia Alsup, Ellen Babb, Mr. and Mrs. Walter Barnes, David Brown, Joseph N. Brown, Eloise Swain Christian, Loretha Cleveland, William and Carolyn Dandy, Vyrle and Mozell Davis, Suzanne Carter Felter, Betty Fuller, Kathryn Fullins, Eloise Gipson Gillian, Nadine Henderson, Annette Howard, Thomas "Jet" Jackson, Bertha James, Elaine Jenkins, Katherine Jones, Willie Mae Harrington McGarrah, Mittie Pounds, Martin Rainey, Gwendolyn Reese, Sandra Rooks, Jacob Simmons, Zanetta Starks, Gerald Syrkett, Jan Vorhees, Mordecai Walker, Alfred Williams, Clarence Edward "Shad" Williams, Faith Williams, Merry Ruthe Wilson, Ophelia Wilson, Eunice Woodard, Henry Woodard and Althea "Jackie" Williams Young.

Finally, we fondly express our gratitude to Becky Wilson, steadfast spouse and friend. She bore up under constant chatter about the progress of this work. More importantly, she guided us through the intricacies of computer programs, image processing and such allegedly basic tasks as burning CDs. Guided? Better to say that she did it for us. We cannot thank her enough.

Introduction

Put down your guns and learn black history. Learn where we came from and who we are.
—John Hope Franklin

One word defined St. Petersburg's historic African American neighborhoods: *connectivity*.

It meant bonding in the sense of neighborhood to neighborhood, household to household, person to person, spirit to spirit. Such ties meant looking out for one another during segregation's harsh days.

Such ties meant mutual survival.

The concept emerged during the era of slavery. In the twentieth century, African American neighborhoods in St. Petersburg, as elsewhere, arose from a need to find self-sufficiency during the Jim Crow period.

In St. Petersburg, that era is defined as lasting from about 1900 until the mid- to late 1960s.

This book is about the African American neighborhoods, which during that period were cut off and kept separate from most of the white world.

It is a companion volume to *St. Petersburg's Historic 22nd Street South*, published in 2006 by The History Press. That book told the story of the city's main African American business, leisure and residential district during the segregation era. This book tells the rest of the story.

It is not always a pleasant one. Violence and terror often rode with Jim Crow. Some of that history is related in this book. The events, however horrific, are recorded as necessary elements in understanding the black experience and in the hope that they never will be repeated.

Residents in Methodist Town and Pepper Town drew strength from one another during this time. Along Twenty-second Street South and amid the teeming streets of the Gas Plant neighborhood, they supported black businesses.

Betty Fuller as a young Pepper Town resident in the 1950s. The houses in the background were typical of Pepper Town, which extended along Third and Fourth Avenues South, just east of Ninth Street (later Dr. Martin Luther King Jr. Street). *Courtesy of Betty Fuller.*

The elite families who lived on Sugar Hill along Fifth Avenue South offered successful role models to youngsters who may have lived in less fortunate circumstances nearby. Almost every adult played a part in raising the neighborhood's children. All respected the idea of common good.

Much of that connectivity disappeared during the second half of the twentieth century. An interstate highway divided communities. More significantly, integration opened new opportunities, allowing people of color to live, shop and spend leisure time where they wished.

Few would wish a rebirth of segregation and its dehumanizing effects. It is important to see that truth in 2008, as many worry that schools in St. Petersburg may be drifting toward a new racial separatism.

Nonetheless, it is ironic that integration—a *connection* in certain ways with the larger society—left in its wake a *disconnection* within the black community in terms of the bonds and lifelines that once assured its survival.

In terms of what has been lost through progress gained, there was a time when—through the generosity of Mother Nature, caring neighbors and families—black people helped each other. There was an avenue of protection from hunger through the unlimited bounty of Tampa Bay and the use of fishing poles. Backyard chickens, fresh eggs and sun-kissed vegetable gardens

Children line up for a special day at the Jordan Park Community Center. This photo is from the 1950s. The man at far right is George Grogan, who booked bands at the Manhattan Casino, managed the Jordan Park housing complex and taught at Gibbs High School. *Courtesy of Norman Jones II.*

provided meals for family, neighbors and friends. There usually was enough to occasionally accommodate less fortunate strangers, family, friends and preachers for Sunday supper.

For ambiance, fresh flowers from household gardens carefully placed in the front room on a table or piano that was covered with a crocheted scarf added comforting touches to the reality of hard times.

Neighborhood fish fries and barbecues provided culinary delights and the opportunity for an exchange of social, mutually beneficial information. Today we wonder: Where have all the mangoes gone? Even during the segregated days of strife, stress, hardship and frustration, it was difficult to find a family whose backyard did not offer fruit trees containing oranges, grapefruit, tangerines, lemons (for sore throats and lemonade), avocado, papaya, a variety of guavas (for jellies and jams), bananas, persimmons and, of course, the ever-present sweet mango and the tangles of vines made heavy by wild grapes.

Every yard had a mulberry tree that provided the main ingredient for succulent pans of mulberry "doobie," a delicious deep-dish dessert that everyone loved.

Even the smallest houses, with little yard space, were hosts to an ever-present supply of collard greens, hot peppers, tomatoes and sometimes sugar cane, providing more than any one family needed. Neighbors visited the sick with a pot of homemade soup. Bereaved families were remembered with food and flowers from the most modest homes of neighbors and friends. If someone's home was destroyed by fire, neighbors supplied a new start, providing curtains, drapes, dishes and anything that could be spared to get the unfortunate neighbors "on their feet again."

In the twenty-first century, there is a lack of the comforting, old feeling of connected community. The price: losing young people to crime and drugs or allowing them to fall short of their potential. It is becoming painfully clear that a disconnected community is, on a larger scale, the twin of a house divided. The community's children are the victims.

This book primarily reflects the experiences of St. Petersburg's twentieth-century residents who experienced Jim Crow's ravages and thrived in spite of the hardship.

But it is hoped that young people will read, come to understand what their elders went through and find a way to restore the best of yesteryear before freedom.

In other words, may they rediscover the old ties—may they learn what these ties meant and how important they were.

And may they forge a new and revised sense of community connection as the new century unfolds.

Mrs. Carrie Singleton, a Pepper Town pioneer, enjoys a pleasant morning on her front porch. *Courtesy of Betty Fuller.*

Chapter 1

The Old Ties

We need history. We need proof for our children. We need history to show the strength of their ancestors.
—*Bill Cosby*

The sun battered relentlessly, slashing through thin pines, hammering a sea of soft, white sand and assaulting in its fury the work crews who found no shade to bless.

White promoters said the tiny Pinellas peninsula, hanging off Florida like a thumb, must be the world's healthiest place to live.

Sweet seawater washed its shores and the soft Gulf of Mexico wind carried the scent of its citrus, they said. It was a place where care would dissolve, they said.

To scores of black men hammering the Orange Belt Railway tracks, all it was, was hot.

During 1887 and 1888, through the steaming gut of the Pinellas peninsula, the men built a lifeline toward the dusty paths and few frail buildings that comprised a hamlet still without a name.

It is notable (and ironic) that African Americans, responsible for the labor that built much of St. Petersburg during its various boom eras, also were a major force in building the Orange Belt, the transportation line that gave the city its start—and eventually brought hundreds of thousands of tourists to feed its resort economy.

Historians credit John and Anna Donaldson and their family as being the first people of color to populate the Pinellas peninsula. Arriving from Kentucky in 1868, the Donaldsons established themselves as capable entrepreneurs who won wide community respect. Some of their descendants still live in St. Petersburg at this writing. Another black man arrived about the same time as the Donaldsons, but his identity has been all but lost by historians. His name

Pepper Town resident Betty Fuller was considered one of the finest dancers ever to grace the Manhattan Casino's ballroom. *Courtesy of Betty Fuller.*

was John Cyle, a laborer who worked for the Donaldsons.[1]

But the men of the Orange Belt were the first African Americans to arrive in numbers.

They worked and lived together, sleeping along the rail bed in makeshift shelters or on the ground. When they finished the job, some decided to stay at the end of the new line. They began settling in an area called Pepper Town, near what would become Fourth Avenue South and just east of what would become Ninth Street (later Dr. Martin Luther King Jr. Street).

Pepper Town thrived well into the 1950s and its remnants survived into the 1960s. The neighborhood's name was not, as many in the white community assumed, derived from the color of table pepper. Instead, said James King who grew up in Pepper Town to become one of the city's first African American police officers, residents named it because most of them grew peppers of all kinds in their yards, gardens, pots and tubs.[2]

Pepper Town residents also established St. Petersburg's first Masonic lodge. It met in a building on what became Eighth Street South and Charles Court. According to Lodge 109's informal history, the lodge began on January 11, 1893, under jurisdiction of the Florida Grand Lodge, Prince Hall Affiliation, an African American organization. It predated by a year the establishment of the St. Petersburg Lodge 139 F&AM, a white lodge.[3]

Pepper Town became the first of several black enclaves established first because of convenience and later maintained because of Jim Crow custom and city government strictures that drew boundaries around African American neighborhoods.

In 1894, Methodist Town began to grow in a corner of what were then the western reaches of downtown St. Petersburg. It sprouted around—and was named for—Bethel African Methodist Episcopal Church. Eventually, it became anomalous as a black neighborhood on the city's north side, which was generally off-limits for black people unless they happened to be working there.

A handful of African Americans lived in another north side area until the 1950s. The neighborhood was not named and it began as a relatively remote country community that rose around a church during the 1920s. It was also near Goose Pond, a fertile, wetland farming area eventually paved over to accommodate businesses, including the major shopping center Central Plaza. Seventh Avenue North and Thirty-seventh Street became the defining intersection for that tiny community, which generally escaped much notice from either the black or the white communities, probably because for years it was in largely undeveloped countryside.[4]

"We knew it was there," said Horace Nero, who grew up near Twenty-second Street South. "It always kind of puzzled us."

Along First Avenue South, originally called Railroad Avenue because the tracks ran down the street, a community of laborers, railroad workers and domestic workers began to rise. Then came fishermen, carpenters, grocers, dairymen, sailors, preachers, teachers, painters and people in many other turn-of-the-century occupations.

The neighborhood's population ballooned. Known as Cooper's Quarters in its early days, it later became known as the Gas Plant, named for two huge cylinders that held the city's natural gas supply. It developed its own business district along Second Avenue South, and was home to Davis Academy, an early school for African American children. Churches bloomed, a movie theater opened and—predating Mercy Hospital, which opened in 1923—the first medical treatment facility for black people was established.

As in other communities, the Gas Plant area had neighborhoods within or close to it: Little Egypt, Sugar Hill and Lincoln Court, for example. Likewise, Methodist Town had Jackson Street, Burlington Avenue and Bolita Alley.

Strict segregation hemmed African Americans into these and other neighborhoods until the 1950s, when black leaders such as Dr. Robert Swain began building beyond white-defined racial boundaries. Swain fought the city for months to win building permits, finally succeeding after threatening to sue the city for violation of his civil rights.

In its earliest days, St. Petersburg apparently did not enforce the harsh segregation that later defined part of the city's character.

Longtime African American resident Paul Barco said his father, who came to St. Petersburg in 1905, believed racial discrimination was less intense early in the twentieth century.

During the 1930s, tenement houses stretched along the railroad tracks near Second Avenue South in the Gas Plant area. *Courtesy of Norman Jones II.*

Said Barco:

My daddy said when he came to this city, if you had to go to a doctor, you went on over to the doctor. He had one waiting room there, he waited on whoever was there. But my dad said as these persons began to come down who had the great amounts of finance and they had been exposed to a great deal of literary training, then these people felt that they didn't care to sit in the same room with these [black] *people.*[5]

Early city directories seem to support the elder Barco's perspective. A 1900 directory does not suggest rigid racial boundaries, although the beginnings of what would become African American neighborhoods can be discerned.

For example, the directory noted that dry goods merchant Charles Parry was "colored." Recorded as being born in England in 1869, Parry lived on Third Street with his family, which included his wife Agnes and eight-year-old daughter Dorothy. Neither Third Street North nor Third Street South has ever been part of a traditionally black neighborhood.

Likewise, Enoch Powell was a thirty-nine-year-old barber of color who lived on Central Avenue (then called Sixth Avenue) with his wife Lottie and four young children.

By 1908, a directory suggests that the African American population—probably at about a thousand—was beginning to locate in sections that were to become identified as black neighborhoods during the segregation era.

Even so, there were exceptions—such as Charles Colyer, a tailor, listed as having a residence at 132 Central Avenue, far outside segregation's usual boundaries.

But pressure had begun to grow to move black people as far as possible from white neighborhoods and the downtown business area.

As early as 1906, vigilantes tried to chase African Americans farther from Ninth Street and Central Avenue. By the 1920s, what would become the city's most important African American business district began to develop along a country dirt trail that would become Twenty-second Street South. It was near an industrial area, and white businessmen recruited black laborers who would live in the neighborhood and perhaps encourage others to move farther from the heart of the city.

Black people found work in St. Petersburg's tourist business, which early in the 1900s began to bolster agriculture as the Pinellas peninsula's major economic base.

But as St. Petersburg began to earn national notice as a leisure kingdom, white business leaders made sure the construction workers, hotel employees, cafeteria porters and domestic workers lived out of sight in neighborhoods where visitors would not see them after working hours.

Neighborhood segregation along racial lines began to be the norm. By the 1920s, it was entrenched as a custom. If the local mores were not enough to enforce strict separatism, violence was a resort—and not necessarily the last one. Receiving implied encouragement from local newspapers, white residents participated in the 1914 lynching of a black man suspected of murder and rape. Later, the city boasted one of the state's largest Ku Klux Klan klaverns, which was always on hand to help intimidate.

The black neighborhoods became havens in the storm, where people could be themselves without needing the approval of whites.

The blessing of friendly, helpful neighbors lightened those troubled times, and in the smaller but still significant scheme of things, so did the periwinkles, roses, life-sustaining gardens and tubs and buckets of asparagus fern that graced front porches.

As if drawing strength from the earth, residents planted vegetables and other greens. They grew everywhere, from the most poverty-stricken neighborhoods to the impressive Sugar Hill homes of St. Petersburg's more elite and influential black families.

Early black pioneer families and their progeny learned, through example from one generation to the next, the coping skills that enabled them to refuse to allow poverty to fester and become a state of mind.

People bathed, washed clothes, dishes and windows, practiced spring cleaning, beat rugs on the backyard clotheslines and scrubbed their floors with water from backyard, porch and kitchen pumps or from water collected in rain barrels permanently placed at the corners of houses.

Monday was "wash day." Adventurous children were allowed to bathe and play in tin tubs of blue-tinged rinse water—the last rinse water before clothes were hung to dry in the sun and a comforting breeze.

For most people in the twenty-first century, such things are faded memories or experiences unknown. Old-timers are amused to see packages of chicken feet in supermarket meat counters as reminders of times long gone when such hors d'oeuvres of today were crisply fried necessities that made the difference between growling stomachs and meatless meals.

White leaders attempted to codify their apartheid ideas with charter changes and city council resolutions in the 1930s, but in practice, the formal codes were unenforceable.[6]

Not until the 1960s did integration begin to take hold in a serious way. Lunch counters, and then entire restaurants, began serving blacks. Old restrictions that kept African Americans from patronizing many white-owned businesses started to evaporate. Separate restroom facilities began disappearing, and most of the "colored only" signs above drinking fountains came down.

The city government hired its first black bus driver in 1964, and four years later, following a court suit, African American police officers for the first time were permitted to patrol all parts of the city, not just black neighborhoods. Court-ordered busing in 1971 assured significant school integration throughout the county.

It was a new day, a long time coming, and for the most part it was welcomed as a step on the road to equality. But it didn't come free.

"Integration will be a good thing, but it's going to cost us," coauthor Rosalie Peck recalls her mother, Octavia Peck, saying quietly. Her clairvoyant proclamation was never more truly manifested than now, more than forty years later.

When the old neighborhoods disappeared—in some cases because they were razed—the old ties were lost.

And with them went the sense of community that for so long had sustained a people, their sense of self and the ever-precious commodity of connectivity.

Chapter 2

Remember the Gladiators

The world is full of the possible, but you have to fight to win it.
—William F. Lampton

They could make a movie.

What the 1966–67 Gibbs High School basketball team accomplished is worthy of inclusion among dozens of screen sports sagas based on actual events—*Rudy*, *Friday Night Lights* and *Hoosiers* come to mind.

Unfolding during a tense era of national social change and a smoldering racial climate in St. Petersburg, the Gladiators' march to a state championship contains drama worthy of the ages. In a way, it defined for an entire community the nature of what was still an all-black high school.

Forty years after the glory, the pride remains, said team member Stepney Johnson. People in the old Gibbs community and throughout the city should remember the Gladiators, he said.

"Honor and be proud of what that school and that basketball team did and how well it represented your city and the state, and what those kids had to go through to get that," he said.[7]

Even before that dramatic season, the battlefields were many. Students at Gibbs had to prove themselves at every turn.

When the school opened in 1927, the African American youngsters had to show they wanted it. They did so by walking with a few teachers several miles over unpaved roads and through fields to move into a building originally meant for whites. Other than some church-affiliated schools, black youngsters could attend only Jordan Elementary and Davis Academy. They had no high school.

Davis Academy, which opened in 1910 and later was named Davis Elementary, was for years the only school for African Americans in St. Petersburg. *Courtesy of the City of St. Petersburg.*

At Gibbs, youngsters learned with secondhand textbooks. They took chemistry in a classroom where a couple of test tubes and one Bunsen burner comprised all of the equipment.

They helped build some of their own facilities.

They excelled, and part of the reason they did was because it was expected by an excellent faculty. Generations later, legendary teachers and coaches such as O.B. McLin, George Perkins, Love Brown and Lewis Dominis are recalled by former students.

So, too, did the community expect excellence from its students.

Scholar Evelyn Newman Phillips suggested that Gibbs represented a genuine alma mater in its role as a nurturing influence, and as such, it became revered in all African American neighborhoods.

Phillips wrote:

> *Gibbs, more than any other institution, gave the African American community a sense of belonging. Churches, social clubs, and neighborhoods divided people by philosophical interests and geographical boundaries but*

Gibbs bonded them through a common experience of education, intimacy, and collective struggle.[8]

Named for Jonathan Clarkson Gibbs II, who became Florida's first African American secretary of state and, later, superintendent of public instruction during Reconstruction, Gibbs High School has yet to see its definitive history written.

When it is, its themes will include the school's status as the beacon that brought a community together. Whether they lived in Methodist Town, Little Egypt, Pepper Town, Forty Quarters, Sugar Hill, Jordan Park or Twenty-second Street South, teachers, parents and students worked together to strengthen what was their major source of pride during St. Petersburg's Jim Crow days.

They bought and furnished the tools to build the school's combined gymnasium and auditorium, which was called a "gymnatorium." Fish fries, sports events and choral concerts helped raise money for construction. Can-do attitudes energized movements to build a cafeteria and then basketball and tennis courts.

Teachers and mentors encouraged such spirit early in a child's life at Davis Academy in the Gas Plant neighborhood, at Sixteenth Street Junior High and at Jordan Elementary.

Youngsters carried to Gibbs a foundation that translated into success in academics, the arts and athletics.

For example, in 1960 Gibbs distinguished itself by becoming the first black school to be accepted into the Southern Association of Colleges and Schools. The honor confirmed that Gibbs, the only African American high school in St. Petersburg, and one of just two in Pinellas County, offered a quality education.[9]

If segregation limited textbooks and equipment, it also offered a community a chance to develop its own school and control its curriculum. Higher math, science, Latin and Shakespeare were taught, but teachers were encouraged to offer African American perspectives on a consistent basis.

Said 1963 graduate Robert Perry, "Our teachers made us realize that we were black and we had obstacles to face and we really didn't have much time to waste."[10]

Accordingly, the faculty made sure prominent people in politics, sports and the arts shared their views and spoke to students. Among them were Eleanor Roosevelt, singer Marian Anderson, pianist Lois Towles, child prodigy and pianist Philippa Duke Schuyler, world champion boxer Beau Jack and Mary McLeod Bethune, who was considered one of the nation's greatest educators.

In particular, Gibbs had a knack for producing talented musicians. Among them were George and Buster Cooper, Al Williams, William Dandy, Sam Robinson, Syl Austin, Frank Royal, Oscar Dennard, Chet Washington, Leonard Graham (better known as Idrees Sulieman) and Chris Styles. Some remain active at this writing.

Teacher extraordinaire O.B. McLin founded the acclaimed Saint Cecilia Chorus of Gibbs High School in 1928. Generations of gifted singers were members. Among them were Cecil Dandy and his gifted siblings, Mae Ollie Keys, Louise Alexander, Nedra White, Eula Bogans, J.B. Smith, I.C. Bryant, Lucille Beckom, Raymond Dickey and James McCoy. They were featured singers who entertained locally and traveled with the choir. In the late 1940s, the chorus came under the direction of Ernest Ponder, who was also a gifted singer. He joined the Gibbs faculty after graduating from Morehouse College in Atlanta. The choir is considered the role model for the widely known Alumni Singers, which was organized in 1980.

Football and basketball teams won state championships and consistent recognition as being among the South's best. N.L. "Love" Brown, football

William Dandy, a talented singer, is shown in his freshman year at Florida A&M University. He became school superintendent in Broward County. Dandy grew up near Twenty-second Street South and Seventh Avenue. *From the private collection of Rosalie Peck.*

These unidentified Gibbs Gladiators are shown practicing at Campbell Park, where the high school team played its games. Legendary coach N.L. "Love" Brown coached these players. This picture was taken sometime during the early 1950s. *Courtesy of Norman Jones II.*

coach from 1939 until 1963, was known as a demanding mentor who cared deeply for his players. Former players recalled that he would drive around the community making sure his players obeyed a 9:00 p.m. weeknight curfew.

"Here comes coach, and we'd strike out running," recalled former player James King. The Gladiators played in what was called the Big Ten conference against teams from Miami, Tampa, Sarasota, West Palm Beach and Daytona Beach. Sometimes they would travel to Georgia to play Bainbridge. They played home games in a dirt and sandspur patch at Campbell Park. Players called it the Dust Bowl.

"Coach had us out there running until it was so dark you couldn't see a hand in front of your face," said King, who still bears a scar under his lower lip from his football days.[11]

Horace Nero, another former player, also remembers well his coach's diligence.

"He caught me out on a porch when I should have been in bed," said Nero, who years later marveled at what he recalled as a "memorable bawling out."[12]

Even Brown's practices were something to see. Scores of people came out to watch the drills and encourage younger players who seemed about to give up. It all contributed to the sense of connectivity Gibbs brought to African Americans throughout St. Petersburg.

But nothing galvanized them like the 1966–67 basketball team.

In mid-autumn of 1966, practice began, and so did one of the toughest journeys a high school team could make.

St. Petersburg, like the rest of Florida and the South, was tiptoeing out of the segregation era. Schools were not yet fully open to children of all races. Some lunch counters and public facilities such as Spa Beach had in theory been integrated, but the city had a long way to go. Most African Americans still remained in segregated neighborhoods; still seen were "colored only" drinking fountains and restrooms; and African American police officers were suing the city government to win the ability to patrol all neighborhoods, not just the black areas.

Meanwhile, all-black schools such as Gibbs played in their own league, separate from the all-white Florida High School Athletic Association.

In 1966, Gibbs became the first black school to compete against the white schools.

Elbert Crumb. Stepney Johnson. Leon Waller. Thomas Daly. Jerome Hillsman. They were the frequent starters.

Some of them grew up in the Jordan Park and Twenty-second Street South neighborhoods. They weren't big kids. But on their slender shoulders, they carried the hope of a community.

Freddie Dyles was the coach. Charles Manning was his assistant.

Emanuel Stewart, a career educator who helped break through other racial barriers in St. Petersburg, was the Gibbs principal.

Together, they created a storybook legend.

During the 1966–67 season, Gibbs compiled a 27–2 record.

In an amazing postseason run, playing in gymnasiums literally packed to the windows behind the high seats, the Gladiators won the state championship for 2A schools—at the time Florida's largest high school classification.

"Everyone knew they could do it. Everyone did not really understand the implications and how it would change history," said Ann Taylor, a former board president of the St. Petersburg Historical Society.

Taylor, the daughter of a pioneer African American disc jockey in St. Petersburg, knew most of the players.

Some of the memories include the racial taunts and ugly names spectators sometimes used.

Emanuel Stewart, a longtime educator, was principal of Jordan Elementary School and Gibbs High School and held numerous other positions in the Pinellas County school district. *Courtesy of Norman Jones II.*

"It was hard, but I didn't pay attention to it, really. Half the time I didn't even hear them," Waller said.

Team members realized they represented a school and a community engaged in a cause bigger than sports.

The team "was an integration breakthrough. It was being used as a tool to test the waters, so to speak," Elbert Crumb said.

Gibbs High School became a community's iconic institution during the segregation era.
Courtesy of the City of St. Petersburg.

One of the more electrifying sports events in St. Petersburg history occurred on December 30, 1966. Gibbs played Clearwater in the final game of a holiday tournament.

All-white Clearwater—considered a rich upcounty school—was a traditional power, ranked number three in the state by sportswriters. Upstart Gibbs was number one.

About seventy-five hundred spectators stuffed Bayfront Center, which was then St. Petersburg's largest indoor sports venue. At the time it was said to be the largest crowd ever to attend a high school game in Florida.

"We had to stop selling tickets," Stewart said. The sales had filled Bayfront to its capacity.

People who couldn't get in waited outside in the parking lot. They could hear a thundering "Whoomp!"—a war cry Gibbs fans shouted whenever a player took a shot or grabbed a rebound.

In the arena, one side was filled with white people; the other, with black people.

"The din was deafening," wrote the *Evening Independent*, the city's afternoon newspaper.

Earlier that day, civil rights activist Joe Waller, who later took the name Omali Yeshitela and founded the Uhuru Movement, had torn down a racially inflammatory mural at St. Petersburg City Hall.

But there didn't seem to be any talk about Leon Waller's first cousin's action. "If there was, it wasn't through me. He was doing his thing, and I was doing mine," said Leon.

The game was "the greatest show on earth," wrote the *St. Petersburg Times*.

Gibbs won 70–66, barely escaping a desperate Clearwater rally.

It represented a breaking down of racial barriers, to the extent that was possible then.

After the game, opposing players shook hands. Some embraced. No incidents among fans were reported.

"There may have been one or two minor things, which I've forgotten about," Stewart said. "They played a good game, and we played a good game, and that's what people came to see."

A couple of months later, Gibbs challenged the best at the state tournament in Gainesville.

The team defeated powerful, physically intimidating Archbishop Curley of Miami, 67–65, in overtime.

The final was almost anticlimactic. Gibbs swamped Jacksonville Terry Parker for the championship, 69–55.

Afterward, Terry Parker cheerleaders posed with Gibbs players and fans for photos. Congratulatory telegrams poured in—including messages from Pinellas County schools Dixie Hollins, Clearwater and Northeast.

The players still try to keep in touch, Hillsman said. At this writing, he is a retired asphalt worker living in Clearwater. Stepney Johnson moved to Los Angeles, where he is an executive with Interscope Geffen A&M, whose musicians include Eminem and 50 Cent.

Leon Waller drove a Pinellas County school bus and is retired in St. Petersburg.

Thomas Daly is retired in Nashville.

Elbert Crumb lives in St. Petersburg and coached basketball at Osceola High School for twenty-four years. He later taught drivers education and physical education at Gibbs.

Freddie Dyles, who coached Gibbs basketball teams until 1993, died at age sixty-six in 1999. Charles Manning died in 1996 at age sixty-three.

Emanuel Stewart retired in 1981 and lives in St. Petersburg. In 1987, he was named the city's "Mr. Sun" for a lifetime of civic achievement. It was the first time an African American had received the honor, which is bestowed annually during the city's spring Festival of States.

In 2006, 1963 Gibbs graduate Minson Rubin, a keeper of community history and a dedicated alumni association member, organized special recognition for the team at an alumni picnic held at Maximo Park.

It was the kind of thing Johnson had in mind when he said the team should be remembered.

"Please don't wash it away," he said. "Honor those trophies."

They stand for connectivity.

The original Gibbs High School alma mater:

Dear old dear old Gibbs High
You're the world to me
Dear old dear old Gibbs High
You will always be
For you bring me sunshine
Everywhere I go
I am always thinking of you
When the shadows 'round me creep
Always thinking of you
When I lay me down to sleep
Dear old dear old Gibbs High
You're the world to me.

Chapter 3

Home in the Neighborhoods

I tell the youngsters if you know where you're coming from it's going to be easier to get where you're going.

—*Quincy Jones*

In mostly flat St. Petersburg, Fifth Avenue South takes a startling dip and climb between Sixteenth and Twelfth Streets. During the segregation era, both its geography and its residential appeal surprised newcomers.

Coming out of downtown, passing busy commercial districts and the crowded, often dilapidated housing of black neighborhoods, motorists saw Sugar Hill rise like a sweet vision of success.

It was a neighborhood within a neighborhood, and its few gracious dwellings represented aspiration and attainment. In majestic stone mansions, stately brick dwellings and well-kept bungalows lived the elite society of St. Petersburg's influential black families, and the area was the pride of St. Petersburg's African American population.

During the segregation era, which in St. Petersburg lasted roughly from the turn of the nineteenth century until the 1960s, most African American residents lived in one of several readily identifiable neighborhoods.

PEPPER TOWN

Pepper Town was situated just east of Ninth Street (now Dr. Martin Luther King Jr. Street) along Third and Fourth Avenues South. It was St. Petersburg's first black community, established when the railroad arrived in 1888. All the original housing stock is gone, although some dwellings from the 1930s and 1940s remain. In the late twentieth century, the area became a diversely populated section of the greater downtown area. By 2006, condominiums had sprouted and further redevelopment is likely. Few single-family homes are left.

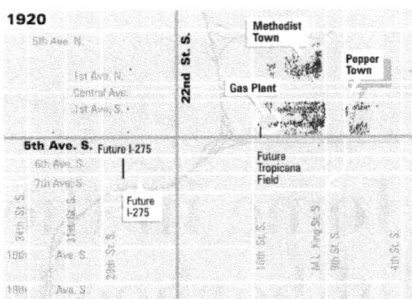

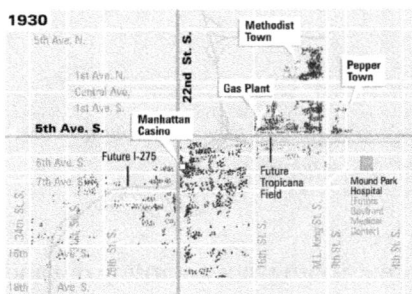

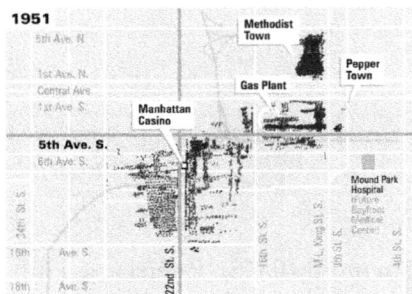

These maps locate the four major African American communities and illustrate their growth rate, the rise of the Twenty-second Street South neighborhood, the dense contraction of Methodist Town and the gradual disappearance of Pepper Town. *Courtesy of Don Morris.*

Methodist Town

Methodist Town was located west of Ninth Street between Arlington and Fifth Avenues North. It began developing about 1894 around the Bethel AME Church—a landmark that is one of the few Methodist Town structures remaining. Methodist Town had its own small business district, and a widely known hotel called the Robert James, which accommodated black entertainers and athletes and boasted a restaurant, ballroom and frequent entertainment.

Gas Plant

The Gas Plant area, west of Ninth Street between First and Fifth Avenues South, was so named because of the two imposing natural gas storage

Resourceful pioneer and Gas Plant resident Annie Kate McKeever sought and received overnight shelter from a hurricane at the fearsome stockade when her two young daughters, Barbara Ann and Willie Mae Harrington, were small children. The family was served breakfast and was treated kindly. *Courtesy of Willie Mae Harrington McGarrah.*

cylinders that towered over the neighborhood. Among its first residents were African American railroad workers who took up residence along First Avenue South, originally called Railroad Avenue. Gradually, the neighborhood spread south, even spilling over Fifth Avenue South into the Campbell Park area. Like Methodist Town, the Gas Plant boasted its own business section. The self-contained neighborhood also boasted the Harlem Theater, numerous churches and two schools—Davis Academy and the privately operated McCray School.

TWENTY-SECOND STREET SOUTH

The Twenty-second Street South business, residential, professional and entertainment district, which included the public housing project Jordan Park and numerous residential enclaves, got its start in the 1920s when black people began moving there to work for nearby industries and because white leaders

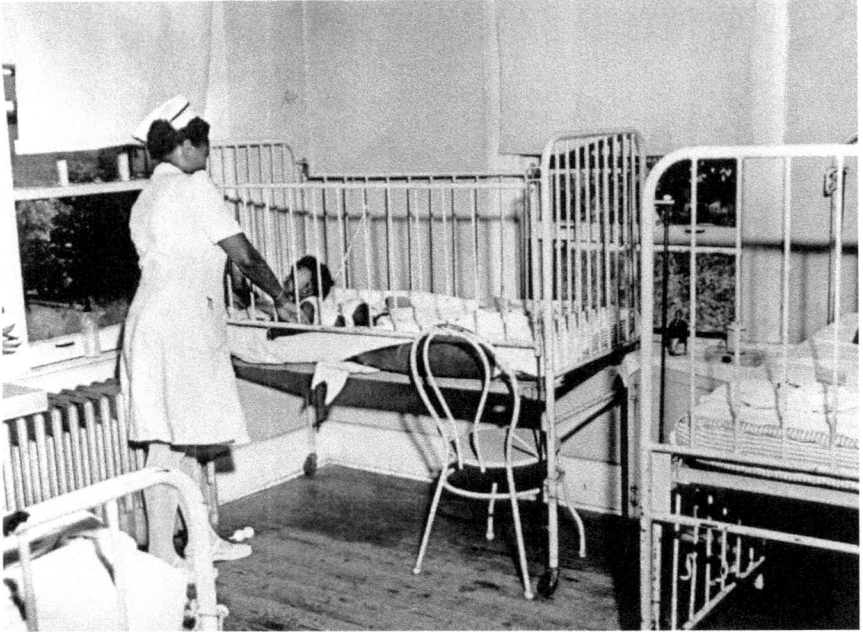

Mercy Hospital on Twenty-second Street South served African Americans from 1923 until it closed in 1966. *Courtesy of the City of St. Petersburg.*

had started prodding people of color to move farther away from downtown so they would not be seen after working hours. Starting as a dirt road in the country, Twenty-second Street between Fifth and Fifteenth Avenues South became the black community's highly charged lifeline, with more than a hundred black-owned or -operated businesses open during the street's zenith about 1960. Louis Armstrong, Ray Charles and B.B. King were among dozens of entertainers who played the Manhattan Casino. The street also was home to the Royal Theater and to Mercy Hospital, a segregated medical facility until its 1966 closure, when the city's hospitals had integrated.

Meanwhile, despite the white-dominated city government's efforts to place strict limits on where African Americans could live, a few pockets of black residents flourished elsewhere, among those locations the area that survived from the 1920s to the 1950s along Seventh Avenue North around Thirty-seventh Street. It was a genuine anomaly, comprising probably no more than twenty people at any one time. It appears to have developed initially around Saint John Baptist Church.

At one time, families also lived in the St. Pete Beach community of Pass-a-Grille.

"We were the last [black] family to leave," said Julius Bradley, who recalled in 1990 that the 1920s boom philosophy, which launched the era of the beach as a tropical paradise, forced African Americans to leave the emergent good life to whites.

Julius's father, William Bradley, owned two houses and a rooming house he rented to black workers from St. Petersburg who worked in Pass-a-Grille. He also owned a concession that sold candy, popcorn, ice cream and cookies, and rented bathing suits to blacks who visited the beach on weekends.

All that had to end.

Bradley said:

> *We had to leave, all Indians and all blacks. It came down from city hall or somewhere. The mayor was named* [J.J.] *Duffy. We were the only ones left. What was happening was the city was expanding, and they were building on the bay side and Gulf side, and the city wasn't going to sandwich in one black family.*[13]

Until integration began taking hold in the 1960s, and even more strongly in the early 1970s, African American neighborhoods in St. Petersburg were isolated and self-sufficient. People who didn't work away from their homes might seldom see a white person.[14] Within the larger neighborhoods, smaller, close-knit residential groupings existed, often identified as "courts" or "quarters," the latter a vestigial term from slavery days.

"Hillary [Clinton] is right. It takes a village," said James King. When he was growing up in the 1940s, the community looked out for its youngsters and shared disciplinary duty, King said. He recalled attending a summer school at Fourth Avenue South and Fourteenth Street in the Gas Plant neighborhood. The teacher, King remembers, was a Mrs. Logan, who one day pinched his ear. The next day, his mother went to see the teacher, learning that her son had committed some minor indiscretion. "My mother said, 'Pinch his ear again!'" King said.[15]

Sugar Hill, probably named for its counterpart in New York City's Harlem, was one of the subdivisions that was part of a larger neighborhood. It was situated on the southern edge of the Gas Plant area.

On that paved and lighted roadway lived doctors, funeral directors and educators. They served as role models for children—and even young adults striving to make their way—who often lived in lesser circumstances just a short walk away, in enclaves such as Little Egypt, Forty Quarters and the Hollow.

Gwendolyn Reese lived on Sugar Hill at 1305 Fifth Avenue South. She recalled that during her early childhood, the entire Fifth Avenue neighborhood enjoyed a close-knit relationship.

"Like an extended family. People felt safe," said Reese, who years later remains in touch with friends from there.

She recalled that Mrs. Phannye Ayer Ponder kept a cherry hedge that Reese and other children of the community loved to raid. Mrs. Ponder founded the St. Petersburg Metropolitan Council, an affiliate of the National Council of Negro Women. Her husband was Dr. James Maxie Ponder, named the city physician for the black population in 1926. He commanded such a measure of communitywide respect that city hall flags flew at half-staff when he died in 1958.[16]

The Ponder home combined modern and old-fashioned conveniences: chickens scratched in the backyard, and the imposing two-story house had a laundry chute and an elevator.[17]

Among other Sugar Hill residents were morticians Edward and Mary "Mae" McRae; Dr. and Mrs. Gilbert Leggett; Dr. Benjamin and Mary L. Jones; entrepreneurs Bill and Essie Williams and Mr. and Mrs. Homer Williams; and educators G.W. and Mamie Perkins, Eloise Perkins, Willie

Inez Dunlap Bynum, *seated*, is crowned the queen of an event at the Melrose Club House by Hester Britten. This photo was taken in about 1950. *Courtesy of Norman Jones II.*

Mae Perkins-McMurray, A.J. and Mary Polk, Mordecai Walker and Anna M. Polk-Walker, J.D. and Julia Brown, Joe Johnson and Mr. and Mrs. Lewis E. Dominis. Longtime residents also included the Herbert Whitehurst family.

Among the more colorful Sugar Hill residents was William Lattimore, who cut a dashing figure at Mercy Hospital, where he liked to stride the corridors and suggest he was the hospital's administrator.

In fact, he was a porter at the Sears store when it was downtown—but he was also much more than that.

"He had more contacts with the people who ran St. Petersburg than anyone else," said Mordecai Walker.

"If I had had any problems at that time, I would not have gone to a lawyer. I would have gone to William Lattimore because of his contacts. He knew judges and lawyers and had considerable access to the powers that be."[18]

Reese said Homer Williams and his family lived in a beautiful, red brick house with artwork, and that Williams invested in real estate. She attended teas at the Ponders' house, and enjoyed watching the Gibbs High School homecoming parade that moved along Fifth Avenue on its way to Campbell Park, where the Gladiators would play their big game long before a field was built at the high school.

Reese's neighbor, Harriet Lee Carlyle, a seamstress, made all of her clothes and also sewed for Inez Haywood when she was a popular Gibbs High School student, and for Mrs. Andrew Polk and her daughter Anna.

Suzanne Carter Felton and her grandmother Ethel Dean lived next door to the Ponders, and Felton said that as a child, she realized the convenience of living next door to a doctor. She said Dr. Ponder was instrumental in recruiting doctors to come to St. Petersburg, including Mrs. Ponder's nephew, Orion Ayer Sr. and his wife Helen. They were the parents of Dr. Orion Ayer Jr. of St. Petersburg, Janice Ayer Jackson of Atlanta, Georgia, and the late Dr. Angela Ayer.

As a child, Felton sometimes spent the night at the Ponder home when the doctor was away on business.

Both Felton and Reese recalled the pleasant ambiance of manicured lawns, clean sidewalks and periwinkles and hibiscus flowers blooming throughout the neighborhood. They remember former neighbors who lived one or two blocks north of Fifth Avenue: Frank Royal and his mother on Dixie Avenue; the Jerome Pittman family; and young Wayne Thompson, an Eagle Scout who grew up to become pastor of First Institutional Baptist Church.

The Harry Cotman family lived on Dunmore Avenue, as did Monroe McRae of the McRae Funeral Home family. The mother of Gibbs High

School teacher Theodore "Moon" Johnson did Reese's hair. Reverend and Mrs. Grant McCray operated a nearby kindergarten to sixth-grade school. Frank Royal, who became internationally known with the famous Buddy Johnson Band, practiced his horn on the back porch of his home, and Dr. B.F. Jones grew beautiful roses.

For the rest of the black community, Fifth Avenue South without doubt stood as an oasis of hope for the less fortunate citizens stranded in an apparently endless desert of race-based segregation.

In 1943, the St. Petersburg city government published the "Proposed Master Plan for the City of St. Petersburg." The city planning commission reported large gaps in the standards of living between blacks and whites, noting that some black people lived without even a toilet in their homes. At least once a decade, either the *St. Petersburg Times* or the *Evening Independent* published in-depth reports deploring housing conditions in African American neighborhoods.

A St. Petersburg city report from the 1930s described, in detail, Methodist Town housing and the lifestyles of many of the people who lived in it. Some

Barbara Harrington Burrell is standing next to a salesman's truck that was making rounds in the Gas Plant neighborhood. This photo is from the 1940s. *Courtesy of* The Weekly Challenger.

maids earned $300 per year; a cook might make $250; and a janitor $700. Entire families were reported as having $500 a year total income. Rent varied—a typical range was $1.25 to $4.50 per week.[19]

But regardless of their circumstances, "poor" was a term that black people refused to accept as a definition of race or persona. This attitude of spirit and individuality explains the proclivity for nice clothes, nice cars and nice homes as far back as the dark days of predominantly rented residences, including shacks. Shotgun houses often were resplendent with neatness from front porch to back porch, surrounded by well-swept sand bed yards. Monday morning laundry days were adhered to, rain or shine. Tubs of flowers and ferns graced front porches, and always, there were tended backyard patches of collard greens, hot peppers and tomatoes.

The late Dr. Johnnie Ruth Clarke, for whom the Johnnie Ruth Clarke/ Mercy Hospital Health Center on Twenty-second Street South is named, used to laugh and say, "You could always tell which family had a little bit more than somebody else by the large tin tubs of fern on the front porch."

Even in ramshackle, overcrowded, crime-ridden neighborhoods without electric power, where outhouses and unpaved streets were common, people pulled together. They worked. Wages were low, but so was unemployment. In 1920, when the census showed St. Petersburg's African American population at 2,444, the black workforce included teachers, grocery store owners, barbers, tailors, ministers, insurance agents, restaurant owners, two doctors, a dentist and a hospital superintendent. They comprised a small middle class at about 6.7 percent of the black working population.[20]

Poverty, of course, was omnipresent. Nonetheless, wrote preeminent St. Petersburg historian Raymond Arsenault, the community was not one of despair. Arsenault continued:

Even its poorest citizens were frequently sustained by strong kinship networks and a vital Afro-American folk culture based on religion and communal values. Single-parent households were relatively rare, and local blacks did not have to look outside their community to find inspiring role models of individual dignity and self-esteem.

Evelyn Newman Phillips did groundbreaking work in her 1994 doctoral dissertation that explored the social history of black St. Petersburg. Included in the work were the recollections of Vanessa Williams, a journalist for the *Philadelphia Inquirer*, who was raised in the Gas Plant neighborhood during the 1950s and 1960s.

Williams said fistfights, shootings, stabbings, alcoholism and teenage parents comprised the bleaker side of life, but that there were also positive elements. Said Williams:

> *Retired schoolteachers would call out to us as we walked to and from school, encouraging us to get good grades and to "Get on home to your mama, now!" Mr. Welch, whose sons included a preacher, teacher, and a tax accountant, would wave at us from his rocking chair on the porch of his firewood business. Another neighborhood character was Miss Callie, an eccentric old woman whose house was filled with toys and games. She would often invite us over for tea parties, during which she'd teach us to be "proper ladies." Neighbors pitched in to feed and bathe the children of single mothers who got sick; the able-bodied cleaned white people's houses and dug ditches during the week, did marketing on Saturday and went to church on Sunday; and my mother grew collard greens and roses in our narrow, sandy back yard.*

Many parents placed a stigma on unwed mothers. Girls from conservative families were not allowed to associate with girls who became pregnant outside of marriage, even if it involved a good friend. Associations were broken on the instruction of parents, who were frightened because the pregnant girls had to drop out of school, thus crushing the elders' goal of education for their children.

Founders Court was a division of the Gas Plant area that old-time residents remember, but Mittie Walton Pounds lived in a subsection few recall.

Mrs. Pounds remembers:

> *Oh yes, the scary gas tanks were there. But the neighborhood within a neighborhood that I grew up in, in the shadow of those big, old tanks, was known as Little Egypt. I lived at 1215 Second Avenue South on the second floor of a two-story house.*
>
> *But even as a child, I dreamed of someday having a house of my own. And I made up my mind at a very young age to hold on to my childhood dream that when I graduated from Gibbs High School and got married, I would marry a man who would build me a house of my own. And I did. And he did.*
>
> *I graduated from Gibbs High School in 1947, married the late Leroy Pounds at Stewart Memorial Episcopal Church when it was still on Ninth Avenue South. And Roy built us a house. And to this day, I am still living in the house that my husband built for us.*

The 1955 house still stands at 3100 Oakley Avenue South.[21]

The thickly populated, rectangular area known as Methodist Town was ironically and uniquely situated in the city's north side, which was generally reserved for whites only. Methodist Town was as tightly controlled as the south side communities, where growing numbers of black people were by custom and city government resolution assigned to live.

It included shacks and tenements, but also a few sturdy, privately owned homes. There was gambling, moonshine and violent crime—but also many churches, house rent parties and black-owned businesses.

The enclave was a short hop from Central Avenue, the highly prized heart of white St. Petersburg, with its historically segregated ordinary and upper-class businesses, entertainment, dazzling theaters, streetcar line and infamous green benches, where only white citizens and tourists were allowed to sit.

In Methodist Town, landlords collected rent from black residents. Many were hardworking people consigned to live in cheap row houses, crowded, wooden, unpainted rooming houses or dilapidated apartment buildings on sand roads with backyard pumps and flimsy outhouses.

Bolita Alley was one of Methodist Town's colorful communities within a community. Long gone by the twenty-first century, any casual mention of it draws raised eyebrows, a smile or two, curious questions and a bit of conversation. For those in the know, the interesting moniker is well understood. Something always was happening there—something worth a story. Maybe it was something violent, or perhaps another intriguing rumor or piece of gossip that had escaped the short street of dilapidated tenements.

Bolita Alley got its name, said Willie Lee Gregory, who was born and reared in Methodist Town, because of the heavy bolita sales and the presence of bathtub gin. Bolita, also called the numbers racket, was an illegal game similar to today's legal lottery. It was based on numbers from the old Cuban lottery and a person could purchase a number for as little as a few cents and hope for a big return if the right number came in.

It was a poverty-stricken section of Methodist Town comprising six two-story, unpainted, wooden, equally spaced row houses for which each family every Saturday paid the owners as little as $1.14 per week in rent. Each house accommodated four families—two upstairs, two down—with a central stairway.

"But there was a lot of togetherness in that neighborhood," Gregory said. "People looked out for each other. And for each other's children."

Gregory also remembered the ice man, a friendly, widely known and well-liked white man who filled iceboxes on a regular basis. He recalled how

These youngsters are taking part in a pageant at the Starling Day Care Center, which has operated in St. Petersburg's African American neighborhoods since the early 1970s. *Courtesy of* The Weekly Challenger.

children played together in games of hopscotch, Chinese checkers, marbles, pick-up sticks and hide-and-seek.

"We played beneath the row houses built high off the ground," he said.

Gregory also recalled the sand beds that burned bare feet, the toilets on the back porches, stoves and lamps lit with kerosene and a common wash shed and clotheslines that all the families shared.

In addition to the rented houses, a few privately owned homes interspersed the neighborhood.

Moonshine was sold in Mason jars and certain houses were known for bolita and white lightning. House rent parties, Gregory said, were common, with Friday and Saturday coming alive with gaiety, music and dancing.

Bolita Alley, said Gregory, was very near his Uncle Bill Gregory's store. From time to time, police poked around, but as a young man he mostly remembers Bolita Alley as a place where people got along with each other.

"I remember it as a place where there was no bickering. It was a close-knit neighborhood. People got along together. We walked everywhere. I remember good times," he said.[22]

The historical relevance of Methodist Town, as with all other historic black neighborhoods of the city, is that despite disadvantages, many of its sons and daughters rose to exemplary heights.

Goliath Davis grew up in Methodist Town. He became the city's first African American police chief and a few years later, the deputy mayor of Midtown, which was targeted by the city for civic improvements. This photo was taken early in his police career. *Courtesy of* The Weekly Challenger.

One of these sons, certainly, is Goliath Davis III, born at home in Methodist Town in 1952. He was delivered by midwife Roxanna Donaldson, who was married to a descendant of early black settler John Donaldson.

Davis grew up on the neighborhood's dirt streets, wearing short pants, no shirt and no shoes.

"My feet were tough," Davis said, noting that the city often sent vehicles around to spray oil on dirt streets and alleys to keep the dust down.

Davis began to learn about life in a barbershop that Moses Cotton operated out of his house. "Buddy Mose," as Cotton often was called, talked

Chester James Sr., the unofficial mayor of Methodist Town, and activist Marie Nesbitt appear before the city council in 1970 to advocate for their neighborhood. *Courtesy of the City of St. Petersburg.*

with his customers about Methodist Town's movers and shakers and its street life, and to the youngsters, about the importance of staying in school.

"You learned a lot of lessons sitting in a barbershop," Davis said.[23]

Davis kept on learning, eventually earning a bachelor's and master's degree and finally a doctorate. He became St. Petersburg's first African American police chief in 1997 after twenty-four years on the force. Four years later, Mayor Rick Baker appointed Davis a deputy mayor, and charged him with rehabilitating some of the historic black neighborhoods south of Central Avenue.

But Davis has never forgotten his roots, remembering Methodist Town as a "rich environment" in terms of its personalities. "It was very much a close-knit neighborhood," he said. "We looked out for each other."

A man who looked out for the entire neighborhood was Chester James Sr. James came to St. Petersburg in 1911 and worked numerous jobs, some of them menial. He was a carpenter, a doorman, a porter and, when necessary, a simple laborer. He helped manicure the yards of such white St. Petersburg luminaries as George Gandy, for whom the Gandy Bridge is named, and C. Perry Snell, an early developer who gave his name to Snell Isle, which is considered one of St. Petersburg's upscale neighborhoods. James also sold fruit from a stand. On Sundays, he played the music in the Tenth Street Church of God.

Ella Mary Holmes, an educator for forty-two years, is the daughter of Chester James Sr., a lifelong advocate of Methodist Town. Holmes is an avid hat collector who once said, "I'll buy a hat before a hamburger." *Courtesy of* The Weekly Challenger.

But he always found time to work for his community, helping his wife Rachel with Methodist Town's first private school. Through the years, he lobbied city hall to improve dark, unpaved streets and to crack down on landlords who neglected the housing they rented to families.

On the civil rights front, James campaigned to register voters, and at age eighty-four he marched with sanitation workers when they went on strike for better wages during the turbulent summer of 1968. The NAACP gave him a distinguished service award during the 1960s, and President Lyndon Johnson honored him for registering a thousand voters.

The city council named James the honorary mayor of Methodist Town in 1974, which was the same year that the council renamed Methodist Town "Jamestown" for the neighborhood's perennial spokesman.[24]

Officials also asked James in 1974 to preside at a city council meeting in which the policymakers approved the construction of town homes in the newly named Jamestown. Passing James the gavel was construed as an honor, but it could be argued that it was an underhanded move to blunt potential opposition to the redevelopment. James later regretted his participation and his vote in the project referendum. It resulted in the relocation of 377 families.

A year later, James told city council: "Had I understood that you intended to take my home, I would never have voted for it. I have never, never, never wanted to get rid of it...We've got nice homes out here."[25]

James kept going at a robust pace virtually until the end of his life. He died of congestive heart failure in 1979 at age ninety-five. He is buried alongside his wife Rachel in Lincoln Cemetery, the burying ground on Fifty-eighth Street South that served African Americans from its opening in 1926 well into the later years of the twentieth century.

Chapter 4

The Business of Life

Good things come to those who wait. Providing you labor while you wait.
—James Bartow Peck

Flagmon Welch had a third-grade education and started a business that put four children through college. William "Bill" Gregory went to the fifth grade and became one of Methodist Town's leading businessmen, establishing several popular enterprises.

They were typical of many African Americans who came to St. Petersburg with little or nothing and pulled themselves up by their bootstraps.

The city's robust tourist economy lured many black people from Georgia, Alabama, South Carolina and other parts of Florida. They saw the opportunity for work that paid better than what was offered by a rural agricultural economy. Between 1920 and 1940, the number of African Americans in St. Petersburg increased from 2,394 to 11,980, according to United States Census figures.

Annie Sue Brinson said her mother and aunt left Quitman, Georgia, in March 1923, bound for new lives in St. Petersburg. They had heard the booming city had opened many jobs.

"Women were attracted by the availability of service work in hotels, restaurants and private homes," wrote Maria Vesperi. They joined the men who came, worked on the railroads, built houses, streets and sewers, stayed and helped erect other infrastructures. Other men worked as garbage collectors, golf caddies, chauffeurs and laborers.[26]

Some became entrepreneurs.

John Donaldson, credited with being the first permanent African American resident of what became St. Petersburg, was one of those—in fact he was the first black businessman, becoming a leading character on what was still a half-wild, nineteenth-century Florida frontier.

Stories of his independence—not to mention his prowess in making money—have come down through generations, both black and white. Early settler John Bethell, who was also St. Petersburg's first published historian, wrote in 1914 that Donaldson, who came here in 1868, was "a man universally respected and one who really kept pace with his white neighbors... He and his wife were respected by all in this section, for honesty and thrift." Bethell wrote from the perspective of having known personally Donaldson and his large family, which included eleven children.

Farmer, woodsman, citrus grower, syrup producer and small-scale cattleman, Donaldson also served as the community mail carrier. He won the job after turning down the postmaster's first offer, declaring that he was "the best off man on this point," even without the mailman's job. He owned property near what became the intersection of Twenty-second Avenue South and Thirty-fourth Street.[27]

Donaldson's work ethic typified that of many other African Americans seeking work in a growing village that soon became a town, and later a small city. They struggled to find their first jobs, worked their way up and eventually started their own businesses.

Flagmon Welch was one of these ambitious men.

Arriving here in 1917 from Alachua County near Gainesville, Welch went to work at any job he could find. In 1922, construction began on the Gandy Bridge between St. Petersburg and Tampa. Welch, a wiry teenager, carried water to the laborers building the span. He earned five dollars a week.[28]

Later, he and a cousin, Herman Welch, started a landscaping business. They collected cow manure from places like Gill's Dairy, which occupied the site later home to Sixteenth Street Junior High—now John Hopkins Middle School. They mixed the manure with dirt and spread the mixture into struggling new lawns in such swanky subdivisions as Snell Isle.

In 1925, Flagmon Welch opened his signature business: Welch's Wood Yard on Sixteenth Street South and Dixie Avenue. When Traveler's Rest Church built its sanctuary on the site, the wood yard moved a couple of blocks to Sixteenth and Fifth Avenue South, where it became a landmark enterprise for half a century.

Open seven days a week from early in the morning until late at night, Welch supplied wood for heat and cooking to black people and white people throughout the city. Customers also could buy rich, black dirt, which Welch often collected from the muck lands of Goose Pond, a marshy area in the middle of St. Petersburg about a mile northwest of the wood yard.

Elder Clarence Welch is pastor of Prayer Tower Church of God in Christ, a church that originated in the Gas Plant area. He is posing with his wife Marilyn. *Courtesy of* The Weekly Challenger.

"On cool days, we'd have cars lined up," recalled a son, David Welch. Sons Clarence Welch and Johnny Welch also were part of the enterprise, sometimes working hours on end.

"From the time we could tote wood, we were working," said Clarence Welch.

Flagmon Welch got the wood from the nearby countryside or from forests miles away. Sometimes, before the Sunshine Skyway Bridge was completed across lower Tampa Bay in 1954, he and his sons would take the Bee Line Ferry across the bay, collect oak and pine in Manatee County and bring it back to St. Petersburg on the boat.

They sold it in twelve-inch pieces for potbellied stoves and in twenty-four- and forty-eight-inch chunks for fireplaces small and large. If someone came with a wheelbarrow, he or she could fill it with wood for two dollars.

Reading the grain of the wood, the elder Welch could take an axe and split logs with the speed and expertise of a lumberjack.

"He could break wood with one whack," Clarence Welch said.

Speaking to a newspaper reporter, Flagmon Welch once said: "I didn't learn when I was a boy, but I know how to work."[29]

He also knew how to raise a family. A deacon for sixty-eight years, Welch taught his children responsibility, honesty, spirituality and unity.

Said David Welch:

> *He certainly gave us encouragement. I remember he was always saying, "I want to make this a better world for my kids, and my grandkids and my great-grandkids." That's all he lived for—his kids. He didn't want them to go through the same things he had gone through.*

William "Bill" Gregory was another entrepreneur recalled as a dedicated family man and friend to all. Gregory and his wife "Bert" were longtime residents of Methodist Town, and operated several much-needed businesses on and near Jackson Street North, including a grocery store across the street from their café, a beer garden and a rooming house.

If you mention the name Bill Gregory to anyone familiar with St. Petersburg's history for the past fifty years, you will hear a typical response: "Oh yes! I remember Bill."

Gregory is affectionately remembered as a man who helped people—a man who literally pulled himself up by the bootstraps and became a successful, self-taught, self-motivated entrepreneur who proved what a man or woman can do in the face of devastating odds.

He was a native of Waynesboro, Georgia, the son of a struggling tenant farmer who, to escape poverty, cotton picking and boll weevils, arrived in St. Petersburg in 1924, only to meet more poverty.

With only a few years of school, compounded by the shackles of racism, he did what he had to do to survive. Sometimes he gambled to make ends meet.

But having been reared with a strong work ethic, the will to survive and a streak of good luck, Gregory put his winnings to good use by opening a lunch room in 1930 on Burlington Avenue North. He later expanded his holdings to a beer garden and hotel. By 1939, he was the proud owner of Bill's Delicatessen at Jackson Street and Third Avenue North, a few steps from both the well-attended Tenth Street Church of God at 207 Tenth Street North and St. Petersburg's popular first and oldest African American church and denomination, Bethel African Methodist Episcopal Church at 912 Third Avenue North.

For forty years, Gregory owned and operated grocery stores on both sides of town: twenty-five years in Methodist Town and fifteen years at a later location on Tangerine Avenue South, where he relocated in 1963 after urban renewal began wiping out Methodist Town.

Through compassion and generosity, Bill Gregory earned the admiration, love and respect of everyone who knew him. His nephew, Willie Lee Gregory, fondly recalls:

> *It was my Uncle Bill who taught me as a small lad to count money.*
> *He gave me my first job washing dishes in the café when I was eleven*
> *or twelve, and as a teenager, a job working in the store. He emphasized*
> *the importance of staying in school. He taught me how to be somebody.*

He proudly added:

> *Bill Gregory was a family man. And he is responsible for my being*
> *the man I am today. But so was his brother, my uncle Leroy Gregory.*
> *They both emphasized the importance of working and saving money*
> *and being honest.* [30]

Bill Gregory attracted the admiration of others as well. "This humanitarian and neighborhood grocer was for the less fortunate, a black minister of food," wrote Peter B. Gallagher of the *St. Petersburg Times* at the time of Bill Gregory's death in 1978.

At the time of his death, his daughter Faye said: "He was a god to me. Another god. He helped everybody and anybody he could in the community. Anybody who needed help knew they could come to Bill."

Despite widespread poverty, affluent black professionals made their mark in St. Petersburg. This yacht belonged to Dr. Robert Swain, an oral surgeon and civil rights activist. *From the private collection of Rosalie Peck.*

Bessie Spivey said at the time:

> *He used to talk about how hard it was in those days for poor people to get food. He told us how he would sell a nickel's worth of rice; a dime's worth of sugar; even sell loose cigarettes for a penny each. If they didn't have any money and they were hungry, he gave it to them.*

Businesses blossomed throughout the African American neighborhoods. By 1925, there were beer gardens, cafés specializing in chicken, taxi companies, funeral homes, an insurance company and doctors' offices. Despite this growing business class, most residents were not prosperous. Few owned cars. Most worked for the railroad lines or in the tourist industry, often as porters in hotels. There were also a few professional men who presaged the numbers of doctors, dentists and lawyers that would hang out their shingles later in the century.

But Alfred "Bill" Williams was a black businessman who had a rare enterprise downtown, and who prospered. In 1929, he started a shoeshine stand whose address was 454 First Avenue North, even though its access was on the alley of an arcade.

He earned money shining shoes for most of the white downtown establishments and their referrals, and city hall for a time considered Williams its link to the black community. In the 1950s, Florida governor Charlie Johns named Williams the state's goodwill ambassador.

During World War II, the South Carolina native won a government contract to shine servicemen's shoes. He employed eleven people. He was able to send three children to prestigious colleges.

Williams had a stroke in 1971 and died three weeks later. His widow, Essie, and a son, Clifford, continued to operate the shop. It wasn't torn down until 1996.

"It was a place out of time," said John Schuh, a longtime patron. "It reminded you of a scene from a [Humphrey] Bogart movie. An institution for sure."[31]

By March 1940, a chapter of the Negro Business League had formed, the *St. Petersburg Times* reported. According to the Methodist Town Pioneers Reunion committee, sixty-eight businesses thrived before 1950 in that neighborhood.[32] At least that many grew in the Gas Plant area and along Twenty-second Street South—city directories show that more than a hundred black-owned or -operated businesses flourished.

The Twenty-second Street entrepreneurs ran groceries and drugstores, furniture emporiums, beer gardens and sundries shops. Doctors, lawyers,

Walter Barnes owned a state-of-the art radio and television shop on Twenty-second Street South. *Courtesy of Walter Barnes.*

dentists and morticians pursued their professions. Beauty salons sprouted. Walter Barnes opened a state-of-the-art radio and television shop, which was unusual in African American neighborhoods anywhere.

City directories from the 1920s through the 1960s help tell the business stories of every neighborhood, not just Twenty-second Street.

Methodist Town boasted, for example, Stokes's Market, J.P. Moses's cleaners and bail bond business, the Harlem Hotel, Marie Nesbitt's rooming house and the Robert James Hotel, owned by Robert Swain, a dentist and civil rights activist. Swain also established the Royal Hotel on Twenty-second Street in the mid-1950s, naming it after the nearby Royal Theater, built in 1948.

Also doing brisk business was the Teen-Age Shoe Shine Parlor, and along Burlington Avenue North, customers came to Lucy Williams's Beauty Shop, Jack's Smoke Shop, the Ace Sandwich Parlor, Bugg's Barbershop, Joe Clark's Sno-ball Shop, Meyer's Laundromat and the Burlington Avenue Market. Others included Dora Small's beer garden, James Gipson's beer garden and Knox Dry Cleaners, which like all others provided services and employment for neighbors, relatives and friends.

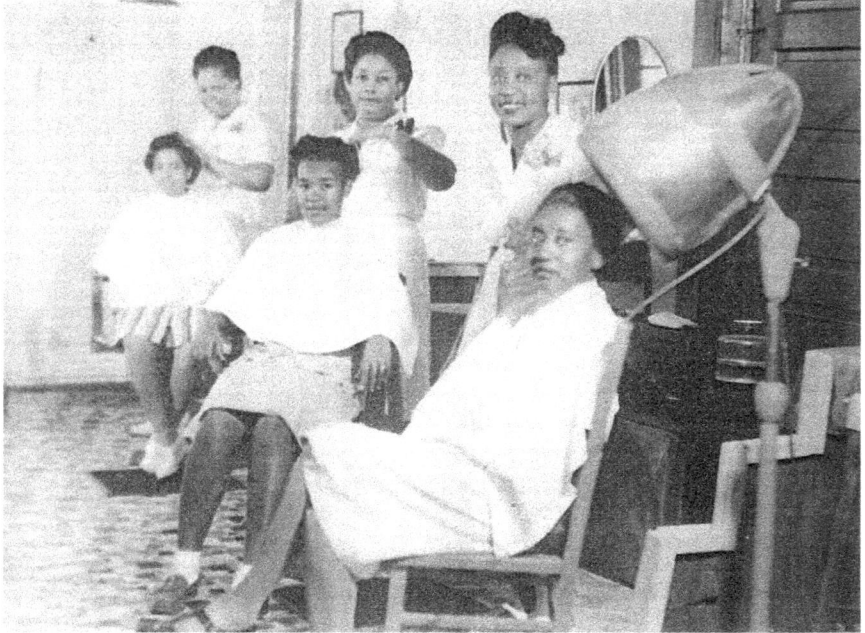

Ethel Bludson, standing next to the hair dryer, operated a beauty shop at 2139 Ninth Avenue South. *Courtesy of Norman Jones II.*

The Gas Plant area offered the Harlem Theater, part of the Florida State Theater chain, but which was a blacks only movie house. The Union Masonic Hall at 1035 Third Avenue South also housed the James Weldon Johnson branch of the public library. Katz Grocery on Third Avenue South was a fixture for years, and was one of a few white-operated businesses in the community.

The Citizens Lunch Counter was legendary for its chicken, and on days steamy or cool, customers could quench their thirst at any of several oases: the Trocadero Café and Tavern, the Silver Moon Bar or Bill's Ron Rico at 938 Second Avenue South, for example.

The "Bill" of the Ron Rico club was Willie Mae Grayson, who came to St. Petersburg in 1924 from Panama City. She and her husband opened their first establishment, a beer garden and café, at 1337 Third Avenue South.

The Second Avenue South spot opened in the 1940s. It also offered a ten-room upstairs hotel, where Pullman porters and visiting baseball players often stayed.[33]

The beer garden café served collard greens, chitterlings, neck bones and corn bread, but also a variety of other dishes. Grayson said she was the first

The Gibbs High School class of 1946 celebrates its tenth reunion at the Robert James Hotel in Methodist Town. *Front row, from left*: Pauline Besselli, Alice Cooper, O.B. McLin (teacher), Gladys Allen, Eloise Perkins (teacher), Verdya Robinson and Eunice Woodard. *Back row, from left*: Ernest Fillyau, Sidney Campbell, Louis McCoy, Lucille Beckom, Ernest Ponder (teacher), Rosalie Peck, Arnold Matthews, Samuel Robinson, Clarence Givens, Willie Woodard and Fred Grayson. *From the private collection of Rosalie Peck.*

African American restaurateur to serve lobster and shrimp as an entrée. Entertainers and baseball players were frequent guests.[34]

Grayson once told a writer that she and her husband were not readily accepted by many churchgoing people when the beer garden first opened.

"We were met with some criticism," she said. "But we had chosen this business to make a living just as a person chooses to be a doctor or a lawyer. We ran an honest business and in time we gained the respect of the community."

Another major business in the Gas Plant neighborhood was Central Life Insurance at 955 Third Avenue South. It was managed by Floyd Dunn, who is recalled as a personable, popular and well-dressed gentleman.

Dunn lived in a well-kept neighborhood immediately south of Jordan Park and just west of Twenty-second Street South. It was an area of privately owned homes heavily populated by professional and business people, including educator and coach, N.L. "Love" Brown, Dr. Robert and Rose Swain, Ernest "Home Cook" Harris and R.C. and Bernice Barnes (who

Robert Creal has owned and operated funeral homes in St. Petersburg since 1955. *Courtesy of* The Weekly Challenger.

frequently were hosts to Buddy Johnson and his sister Ella Johnson when they played the Manhattan Casino).

Residents also included George and Edith Grogan, the Goldie Thompson family and James and Rosa Bond. During segregation, James Bond served as the superintendent of Pinellas County's black schools and maintained an office in Jordan Elementary School. Among other residents were Ethel Bennett, her daughter Ruby and sister Marigold McIver (all schoolteachers), businessman Handy Abrams, Columbus and Gussie Strong Wilkerson, Mr. and Mrs. George Jones and the Richard Smith Sr. family.

Don McRae, a military veteran and high-ranking city government staff member during the 1990s, still has the funeral home his great-uncle Edward McRae started in the 1920s. Robert Creal has operated funeral homes for half a century.

Among other businesses with great longevity in the African American community is *The Weekly Challenger*. The late publisher Cleveland Johnson, a St. Petersburg native, bought the newspaper in 1967 from M.C. Fountain, who at the time owned the only black printing business in Pinellas County.

Cleveland Johnson was the longtime publisher of *The Weekly Challenger*. Johnson died in 2001. His widow, Mrs. Ethel Johnson, is president, and she has continued operation of the paper since her husband's death. In 2007 the paper celebrated its fortieth year of chronicling African American lives in St. Petersburg and elsewhere. *Courtesy of* The Weekly Challenger.

Widely recognized publicist Norman Jones Sr. for a time shared an office with Johnson on Twenty-second Street South.

During his first two decades of ownership, Johnson expanded the paper from a few pages to thirty-two, eight of them in color and seven with full-page advertisements. It circulated throughout the Tampa Bay area and as far north as Inverness, Dunnellon and Ocala, boasting a subscriber list of more than forty-three thousand. William Blackshear was the advertising manager. When Johnson died in 2001 at age seventy-three, his widow Ethel Johnson stepped in as publisher. The newspaper celebrated its fortieth anniversary in 2007.

The Weekly Challenger has thrived as a folksy paper that publishes news that the larger daily papers often miss or ignore. It has always included a large section devoted to news of churches and religion, and Johnson saw to it that feature stories often highlighted new businesses in the community. He also introduced a column written by youngsters. The paper followed closely events related to school desegregation. It kept up with national corporations, noting which ones would hire black employees.[35]

Norman Jones Sr. was a publicist, columnist and radio personality who forged a national reputation. He once had offices on Twenty-second Street South. His papers are stored at the University of South Florida St. Petersburg. *Courtesy of Norman Jones II.*

Known as "Cleve" to his friends, Johnson was popular not only for his business acumen but also for his generosity. He contributed regularly to the Ebony Scholars program for youngsters, made sure that single mothers had nice clothes to wear to work and often gave youngsters paper routes to earn their first money. He also was known for helping out friends in financial trouble. When he died, obituaries were published in newspapers as far away as Honolulu, Hawaii.[36]

Many African Americans worked in construction trades. In fact, it was the reason many came to St. Petersburg. The building industry offered many jobs during the city's boom phases in the 1920s and again after World War II, so it was certain that some of these ambitious men would strike out on their own.

Among them was Mose Reese, an industrious businessman, a popular builder of homes and vast property owner whose own home vanished with the coming of Interstate 275. Reese's wife Mabel was a cosmetologist who taught beauty culture at the Gibbs vocational school. Reese taught his son,

Mose Reese, *left*, was a homebuilder who passed along the trade to his son John L. Reese, *right*. Mose Reese built many of the houses in their neighborhood just west of the Gibbs Vocational School. *Courtesy of* The Weekly Challenger.

of Thirty-fourth Street South, where today reside daughter Mozell and her husband Vyrle Davis, both educators.

John Clayton liked the idea of building businesses. His first jobs working for someone earned him fourteen to eighteen dollars weekly. He decided he would be better off as an entrepreneur. At age twenty-seven in 1938, he bought his first grocery store, and by 1944 he purchased the entire corner of Fairfield Avenue South and Twenty-first Street, where the store stood. He later built three houses on the property.

Despite frequent success, business for African Americans often was difficult. Sometimes entrepreneurs were directly attacked. Brodley Bass, a prosperous businessman, was tarred and feathered three times, apparently because he was well-to-do and was seen as having risen too high for his presumed station.

Community lore also tells of a contractor who won a construction bid, completed the job, went to pick up his money and was never seen again. Evelyn Newman Phillips wrote that members of the community suspected that he was killed because some whites considered him a threat.

There was no investigation.[37]

Chapter 5

Battling Jim Crow's Terrorists

Life is sometimes cold. Go through it. Be like the blackberry. Endure and survive for the sweetness that follows the onslaught of a brutal, merciless winter.

—*Rosalie Peck*

Even with World War I flaring across the ocean, it was a sweet 1914 in St. Petersburg. Optimism buoyed the growing city, which was beginning to come into its own as a resort and perhaps a place to find a good life.

A fine new theater called La Plaza, a second railroad, a new library, a soon-to-arrive spring training baseball team and expanding prospects of prosperity made important men smile. Most of the expanding amenities were of course not available to people of color.

During a mild November a few days before Thanksgiving, St. Petersburg experienced its darkest days and nights.

In a spasm of hate and violence, a white mob lynched a black man.

Walter Fuller, an old guard St. Petersburg businessman, developer and author, described the episode as "disgraceful...a lynching turned into a public spectacle and a complete breakdown of law in a civilized society."[38]

Not everyone in St. Petersburg condoned the episode, although many prominent people did. Those who dispensed the vigilante justice placed the city among many locales that used lynching as a method of intimidating blacks and maintaining white-sought racial superiority. The practice or threat of it was used as a means of social control and to enforce racial division.

Segregation carried with it the lash of swift reprisal when African Americans stepped beyond the boundaries that custom and law decreed. Despite its benign image as a sun-splashed resort, St. Petersburg concealed not far beneath its calculated, carefree surface a subculture unafraid to use violence as a threat and a weapon to maintain white supremacy. In the

1920s the Ku Klux Klan established one of Florida's largest klaverns, whose members rode floats in the annual spring Festival of States parade and bought newspaper ads to recruit members for its youth auxiliary.

There were some in the dominant society that didn't believe in promoting fear. In fact, entrepreneur John Clayton, who was well aware of institutional racism, said that when he was a child in the 1920s, "white and black people got along better than a lot of people thought they did."

He cited a "Mrs. Cooper," with whom he spent his days at age nine. He worked for her around the house and said the two formed a mutual bond of affection. Said Clayton:

> She bought me knickerbockers pants, black socks and shoes and told me to keep those shoes shined...I would answer the door bell, page the person who was coming in, help her clean up and wash the dishes...She sent me home every night carrying a big old pan with everything they cooked and was left over. She gave me a dollar a week and 10 cents every Saturday to go see a movie. A dollar was big money at that time [1922]. I hated to leave her. She treated me so nice.[39]

But Jim Crow's enforcers didn't hesitate to hand out vigilante justice when black men were suspected of crimes, petty or otherwise. Old newspaper files testify to beatings, mutilations and hangings. Old-time residents recall the Klan marching through neighborhoods to intimidate and terrify the African Americans living there. Sometimes they killed black men.

Law enforcement, meanwhile, restricted the movement of black people, especially after dark, and enforced racially based curfews. If you were a young, black man, it was easy to get into trouble. Petty crime often resulted in a harsh response. For example, whites would not hesitate to shoot at a black person for so slight an offense as stealing fruit. Such reaction further defined a system that placed blacks in an inferior position that rarely accorded them the same consideration that would be given to a white person.

Lula Grant, who came to St. Petersburg in 1908, expressed it this way: "It's too bad to say, but we were just black people, and they were white people, that's all. We weren't considered in any way, we were just black people."[40]

The racial climate was why adults in all neighborhoods tried to look out for all youngsters, even someone else's children—it was a matter of protecting them. "Safe havens" were part of the mutual ethic; for example, young men might scoot their cars into handy, open garages if some traffic infraction, however minor, or their presence in a white neighborhood had caused the police to chase them. Drivers considered it more prudent than allowing themselves to be pulled over.

According to residents who remember the Jim Crow era, safety offered—when needed—was part of the survival mechanism and it provided another kind of connectivity.

Sometimes there wasn't much even the most cautious residents could do. On at least two occasions, mobs killed black men.

In 1905, a black man named John Thomas knifed to death the city's police chief, James J. Mitchell. A mob stormed the jail, climbed to Thomas's second-story cell and, as historian Walter Fuller wrote, "shot him to pieces." Then the mob kicked down the jail doors and its members cut and stomped the body.[41]

A lynching episode occurred in 1914 when popular photographer Edward Sherman was murdered and his wife robbed and assaulted. White posses combed St. Petersburg and other parts of Pinellas County looking for two black suspects. One, though never positively identified, was taken from the city jail, marched to Ninth Street and Second Avenue South and hanged from a light pole near Cooper's Quarters, part of what would become the Gas Plant neighborhood. Men, women and children poured a fusillade of gunshots into his dangling body.[42]

It is an unpleasant story whose retelling suggests the stark, feckless brutality latent in a strictly segregated social system in which one group, led by its most prominent citizens, maintained virtual birth-to-death dominance over another group they viewed as less than human. It suggests why no such system can be allowed to survive.

Lynchings were not uncommon, and the ones in St. Petersburg were part of a larger pattern. Between 1882 and 1968, 4,743 people were reported lynched in the United States, and 3,446 were black. In 1914 alone, Tuskegee Institute reported that 51 of 55 lynching victims were black. The *Crisis*, a NAACP magazine, reported even more victims that year—74, of whom 69 were black. In Florida that year, mobs lynched 5 blacks and no whites.[43]

The events that led to St. Petersburg's 1914 lynching began on the evening of November 10, a Tuesday. Ed Sherman had gone to bed about 8:00 p.m., sleeping in a bedroom alcove with low, narrow windows on both sides and two larger ones in the front. Mrs. Sherman was sitting in an adjoining parlor, making Christmas baskets out of grass and pine needles.[44]

The Shermans lived on a remote stretch of Johns Pass Road, later called Thirtieth Avenue North. It was a few yards west of the Atlantic Coast Line Railroad tracks. Sherman had purchased the property three years earlier, and like many others, he wanted to make a fortune in Florida real estate.

From left, Barbara Ann Harrington Burrell and her sister Willie Mae Harrington McGarrah were young residents of the Gas Plant neighborhood. In the left background is the stockade, where African American men often were incarcerated. *Courtesy of Willie Mae Harrington McGarrah.*

During the winters of 1912 and 1913, Sherman and his wife lived on Central Avenue in downtown St. Petersburg, where he had a photography studio. Each summer, the couple returned to Sherman's photo studio in Camden, New Jersey, just across the Delaware River from Philadelphia, where much of the money fueling St. Petersburg's early, small land boom originated.

Sherman hoped affluent Northerners would want to purchase land in Wildwood Gardens, a fanciful name he gave to his property. He called it the "newest suburb of St. Petersburg." Actually, the land still had to be developed. It was several miles from downtown and at least a half mile from its nearest neighbor—out in the country, in fact.

But the photographer-turned-speculator had eleven black men clearing the land and Sherman had built his one-story frame bungalow on the site.

At about 10:00 p.m. on November 10, a blast shattered the peaceful night. Mrs. Sherman ran toward the bedroom where her husband lay. She said that was when a black man stuck a gun in her face, demanded money and threatened to kill her. She handed over about a hundred dollars that her husband had withdrawn from a bank the day before. Mrs. Sherman told police a second black man appeared, and that the pair dragged her outside, beat her with a piece of pipe and tore off some of her clothes. Newspaper articles the next two days strongly implied she was raped. The men fled and Mrs. Sherman said she fainted.

When she came to, she touched her dead husband's cold corpse and fainted again. She told police that it wasn't until 3:00 a.m. on November 11 that she had recovered enough to crawl out of the house and stumble through the woods to a neighbor who, like the Shermans, had no telephone. In a kind of relay, neighbor boys passed the word through one remote house after another until one was found with a telephone. Police were notified and word of the incident began to spread throughout the community, which was stunned by the news.

A shotgun blast had blown Sherman's skull away. His wife lay in Augusta Memorial Hospital and was said to be hovering near death. Newspapers helped ignite community outrage. The *St. Petersburg Independent's* front-page headline read "Slain As He Slept By Unknown Negro." The morning paper, the *St. Petersburg Daily Times*, published photos of Sherman and a black man said to be the assailant. The paper headlined its story: "E.F. Sherman Is Brutally Slain While He Sleeps," and "Two Negroes Accused of Most Atrocious Crime Here in Years."[45]

The November 10 *Independent* had published an editorial just a few hours before the crimes, declaring that St. Petersburg appeared headed for great good fortune, and indeed, there appeared to be reason for optimism. A new gas plant and a garbage incinerator were almost finished. A second railroad was building a twenty-thousand-dollar depot and was expected to begin St. Petersburg service soon. Meanwhile, the Atlantic Coast Line Railroad, already serving St. Petersburg, was heavily promoting the city. A Carnegie grant paid for the new library under construction, and in 1915 the Philadelphia Phillies had agreed to come for spring training.

This was the economic context in which the Sherman episode took place. The social context, in addition to the overarching segregation, included an even more powerful theme: in that place and time, as throughout the South, white women were strictly off-limits to black men, many of whom had died for words or actions perceived to be threatening or insulting.

Suspicion fell immediately on John Evans, a black man who came with Sherman from Dunnellon a few weeks earlier. Evans had worked for Sherman as a chauffeur who also performed whatever odd jobs his employer required. Sherman fired him on November 7 for unknown reasons. No serious quarrel had been reported, but an acquaintance said Evans seemed to carry a grudge. Soon after she regained consciousness, Mrs. Sherman told police she thought she had recognized Evans's voice during the assault.

Police chief A.L. Easters ordered Evans arrested, but when he was taken before Mrs. Sherman, she could not identify him as her attacker. A second man, Ebenezer B. Tobin, also was arrested and held at the new county jail in Clearwater, despite the arresting deputy's claims that he didn't believe Tobin had been involved. Sheriff Marvel Whitehurst kept news of the arrest quiet to avoid mobs storming the jail.

Instead, crowds dashed wildly around St. Petersburg on November 11 looking for suspects, and grim groups scoured dense woods north of town, determined to find the guilty persons. St. Petersburg's commissioners ordered saloons closed, but Central Avenue remained crowded until midnight as white residents pursued rumors that further fueled their agitation. Black people disappeared from the streets, even in their own neighborhoods. Ninth Street was deserted in front of Cooper's Quarters.

The worst was to come.

On November 12, a Thursday, posses raided black homes early in the morning and took a half dozen men to jail. One posse fired three shots at a black man walking alone on Ninth Street.

An estimated hundred armed men surrounded Augusta Memorial Hospital, where they intended to prevent the escape of any suspect who might be brought before Mrs. Sherman.

Many African Americans left the city. Some took the train, while others trudged north along the Atlantic Coast Line tracks, hoping at least to get away from St. Petersburg if not to absolute safety. During the days of chaos, 179 black women and children were reported to have left on the afternoon boat to Tampa, and others took smaller boats to Pass-a-Grille.

The newspapers devoted much space to detailed, often gruesome accounts of the crimes. Articles described the black suspects and reported the progress of the manhunt. The *Independent* published an article that said "the general feeling is that the guilty man should be hanged promptly as soon as positively identified."

Word had reached northern sections of Pinellas County, inflaming residents there. Angry men came to St. Petersburg, some on horseback.

Raiding a house in Methodist Town where Evans had roomed, a search party found a shirt and bloody shoes, which another resident at first said belonged to Evans. He later changed his mind, but it was enough to send the party after Evans once again.

After being released the day before, Evans went to work for a black man along Fifth Avenue South near what would become Twenty-second Street. Someone telephoned his whereabouts to police chief Easters, who gave the posse directions. The caller also said that Evans declared that he would not run from the mob.

When the posse found him, its members nearly lynched him on the spot. Evans still refused to confess. He was taken to Roser Park, an elite white neighborhood not far from Pepper Town and not far from the hospital, where he was eventually brought for the second time before Mrs. Sherman. Again, she could not identify him, saying her glasses had been broken in the assault.

Evans was then placed in the St. Petersburg jail.

During the afternoon, the people crowding downtown seemed to be growing more unruly. "A number of strangers, probably from the outlying sections, appeared and the crowd became more determined," commented a story in the morning *Times*. The account noted that there was no talk of lynching or breaking into the jail. But at one point, a group at city hall became so demonstrative that Mayor James G. Bradshaw mounted the steps to plead. According to an article in the *Tampa Tribune*, Bradshaw contended that he had no doubt that the law would be carried out, whether by summary justice of some determined posse or, as he said he hoped, by a duly constituted court.

At about 10:30 p.m. a mob estimated at fifteen hundred stormed the jail. Accounts vary as to how its members entered. One report said a crowbar was used to pry open an iron door leading to cells; another said bricks were removed from the walls; a third declared the jail walls were battered down; a fourth said ropes or chains hooked to horses were used to tear away the jail's alley door.

The crowd was armed to the teeth and carried guns of all kinds. Someone nearly killed jailer E.H. Nichols. A man thrust a pistol into his face and pulled the trigger, but fire chief J.T. McNulty grabbed the weapon and its hammer fell on the skin between his thumb and forefinger.

Men dragged Evans out and put a rope around his neck.

Then a procession started down Central Avenue from the jail at Fourth Street and Second Avenue South. People poured out of hotels and guest houses, joining the march. Women and children walked along with men. A lighted street car followed the procession, and behind it moved a line of automobiles, motorcycles and bicycles.

Luther Atkins witnessed the episode as a youth and described it years later:

> [Evans] *never said a word. He knew that he was guilty, and he knew it was his time, and as far as I know I never heard him say any sound and everybody was quiet walkin' down the street. And everybody was determined to do one thing, and that one thing was to lynch that* [man], *and that's what they did. It was just that simple. However pitiful it was and unlawful.*[46]

The mob turned south on Ninth Street, stopping at Second Avenue South, where a Cooper's Quarters tenement loomed over the scene. Someone suggested setting fire to Evans, but since the rope already was around his neck, it was decided to proceed with the hanging. Mob members experimented with several poles and trees, finally deciding a light pole would do. News accounts said a boy climbed up the pole's spikes and threw the rope over a crossbar. Mob leaders began hoisting Evans off the ground.

As Evans tried to wrap his legs around a pole, a white woman in a car fired a shotgun into him. It set off a ten-minute volley of bullets and shotgun pellets fired, according to witnesses, by men, women and children.[47]

On Friday, November 13, tension continued to grip the city. White residents talked of storming black neighborhoods again. Angry black residents talked about retaliation. Florida Governor Park Trammell offered to send troops to maintain order. Officials declined, but an infantry company stayed on alert in the armory.

Gradually, calm returned.

A coroner's jury viewed Evans's body at a Central Avenue undertaking parlor and reached a verdict. Evans, the jury said, had died at the hands of parties unknown—despite the likelihood that any number of white citizens had recognized the lynchers. But such verdicts were typical of lynching everywhere. African Americans had very little say in holding public office or serving on juries. Lynchers almost always went unpunished.

As the excitement died away, the city's financial elite must have sighed in relief. It would not have been a good thing to have had killers on the loose and armed bands of men prowling the county. St. Petersburg wanted to impress refined, wealthy Northerners, and Northern newspapers were following developments. Moreover, the dead man's partner, prominent in the Philadelphia area, was coming to see about the situation firsthand.

Rumor, a speculative press and circumstantial evidence had made John Evans available. Few people would object to his killing. St. Petersburg could return to the pursuit of prosperity; its men would quit worrying about the safety of the community.

Several elements suggest the lynching was well organized. On the afternoon of November 12, a policeman visited white people living near the black area along Ninth Street South and warned of impending trouble that night.[48] The coroner's jury convened that afternoon, hours before the lynching, when there was no official reason to meet.[49]

Finally, J.P. Walsh, Sherman's partner, told the *Camden Courier* in New Jersey that Evans had been tried and found guilty during a secret meeting of a committee composed of fifteen of St. Petersburg's wealthiest citizens.[50]

Their identities never were revealed.

Ebenezer Tobin, the other suspect, eventually was identified by Mrs. Sherman. He was tried for murder on September 17, 1915. After deliberating fifteen minutes, a jury found him guilty. Circuit Judge O.K. Reaves sentenced him to be hanged. At 11:06 a.m. on October 22, Tobin died, maintaining his innocence, in Pinellas County's first legal hanging. Sheriff Marvel Whitehurst, who had seen to it that Tobin was kept from the mobs, dropped the gallows trapdoor. Tobin's family would not take the body and it was buried in a potter's field.[51]

Chapter 6

Helping Build Community

Service to others is the rent you pay for your room here on earth.
—Muhammad Ali

Twelve African American police officers did a stunning thing in 1965. They sued their employer, the City of St. Petersburg, to win the right to arrest people.

"We were black men bucking the system," said Primus Killen, one of the twelve.

Because the officers were black, they could not put a white person in jail. They could not patrol anywhere but in black neighborhoods.

Besides its demeaning symbolism, the practice handcuffed black officers' careers. It made it difficult to gain experience in duties other than the gritty, routine work of keeping peace on some of the toughest streets in town. But in St. Petersburg in 1965, it was city policy.[52]

Both white and black people picked up the fact and flung it like a rock. You're nothing but half a cop, the insults implied.

"Hearing that from our own kind...I'd be lying if I said it didn't affect me," said Horace Nero, a black officer who joined the force in 1962 and spent forty years on the job.

With an idealistic young lawyer named James B. Sanderlin leading the way, the suit took three years to play out. When it was over, black officers could patrol the entire city and arrest anyone.

The officers who fought to win full law enforcement duty weren't the first black officers in St. Petersburg. Those pioneer policemen, hired in 1949, included Louis Burrows, Sam Jones, Titus Robinson and Willie Seay.

Nor are they the only ones who broke barriers to serve their community, and the larger community of St. Petersburg. Many, such as C. Bette Wimbish,

Primus Killen was among the police officers who in 1966 sued the City of St. Petersburg for the right to patrol all areas of St. Petersburg, not just the black neighborhoods. *Courtesy of* The Weekly Challenger.

Goliath Davis, Douglas Jamerson and Chester James Sr., are mentioned elsewhere in this book.

Often overlooked is Clinton C. Falana, a Methodist Town resident who liked to be called "Deacon." He became St. Petersburg's first African American bus driver in 1964, an era when the city was beginning to emerge from years of segregation. Dr. Gilbert Leggett, a staunch civil rights activist, had pressured city hall into accepting black applicants and Falana took the test. He worked for more than twenty-five years and earned numerous awards for safe and courteous driving. When he started, he earned $1.60 per hour.[53]

During holidays he and his wife prepared an enormous meal and invited to their home community members who would otherwise be alone. "One year we had 114 people: 8 were blind, 4 were in wheelchairs and 35 or more were above sixty or seventy years of age," Falana said.

The meal is reminiscent of another woman who started a Thanksgiving Day feast that has become a St. Petersburg tradition.

Rosa Jackson in 1973 was sitting alone on her porch at her home near Campbell Park. Recently retired, she was feeling lonely. As she said many times, she had a vision in which the Lord told her to put on a Thanksgiving meal.

C. Bette Wimbish, a lawyer, became the city's first African American city council member in 1969. Her husband, Dr. Ralph Wimbish, was a civil rights activist. *Courtesy of* The Weekly Challenger.

Douglas Jamerson was elected to the Florida House of Representatives in 1982. Governor Lawton Chiles later named him state education commissioner. *Courtesy of* The Weekly Challenger.

So she did.

The first year, fifty people showed up. The next, seventy-five arrived. After a while, the crowd grew too large, so Jackson moved the banquet to nearby Campbell Park Recreation Center. At first, she paid out of her own pocket, but donations of cash and food eventually began to help.

When Jackson died at age seventy-two, her family decided to continue the tradition. Eloise Jones, a daughter, has been the main organizer. She also does the shopping. Darryl Jones, a grandson, typically cooks at home for two and a half days. The menu might include eighteen turkeys, five hams, string beans, collards, mixed vegetables and punch. Up to three hundred people have attended, and a few meals are delivered to people who can't get out.

The feast has remained open to anyone lonely who wants a dinner.[54]

Thomas "Jet" Jackson, not related to Rosa Jackson, has spent a lifetime making young lives better. At this writing, he is a high-ranking member of the city government's leisure services department, which he has been a part of for forty-seven years. He is "Mr. Recreation" for the African American community.

Jackson, who as a youngster won four state diving championships, learned how to swim at Wildwood Recreation Center's Jennie Hall Pool. Later he became a lifeguard there. He credits the late Ernest Fillyau, another community leader, with arranging both those life changing events.

Later taking on supervisory roles at Wildwood, Jackson helped build the center's reputation as the most competitive spot to play basketball in St. Petersburg. He worked with his good friend Ken Robinson to organize tournaments that attracted the best high school, college and amateur players from Florida and beyond. Coaches came to watch and recruit. The professional National Basketball Association used Wildwood as a venue to train officials. Some observers called it "the basketball capital of the world."

Jackson sometimes ran a "midnight madness" tournament, which started at midnight and continued through the next day. It was credited with bringing youngsters off the streets and keeping them out of trouble.

Charles Williams, a longtime friend and former football teammate at Gibbs High School, said this of Jackson: "He spends all his time helping other people. Since he was a young boy, he was always into stuff to help the neighborhood. Every hour of the day, he finds something to do with it."[55]

Like both Jacksons, literally hundreds of people have stepped forward to give time, energy and money to their community. The few mentioned in this book are representative of many others whose stories remain to be told.

Thomas "Jet" Jackson became a popular recreation supervisor in the African American community. *Courtesy of* The Weekly Challenger.

The police officers who sued the city almost certainly forged the most unusual story. Observers thought their suit might be unique in the Southeastern United States, if not in the nation.

During a contentious era of strikes, assassinations and counterculture protests, the landmark civil rights case earned scant attention then and languished nearly forgotten for years afterward.

But many ranking black officers in 2007 remember the men they say helped pave the way for African Americans in law enforcement careers: Adam Baker, Freddie Lee Crawford, Raymond De Loach, Charles Holland, Leon Jackson, Robert Keys, Primus Killen, James King, Johnny B. Lewis, Horace Nero, Jerry Styles and Nathaniel L. Wooten.

"I consider these guys to a certain degree heroes. Any time you have individuals who will stand up for what they believe and go against the institutional, unfair policies, I think that's heroic," said Cedric Gordon, who joined the St. Petersburg force in 1980 and in 2007 was an assistant police chief.

"We were all homegrown kids out of the rough neighborhoods of St. Petersburg, and now we had these shiny blue uniforms on," Baker said.

It reminded him of something heroic. "Like having black cowboys," said Baker, whose name led the list of the twelve plaintiffs in the suit. They came to cherish the nickname of "Urban Buffalo Soldiers," a reference to the black United States cavalry units that formed after the Civil War and saw tough duty on the American frontier.

Many of the young officers who stood together in 1965 knew one another as youths. They grew up during the 1950s in or near Twenty-second Street South or in Methodist Town, Pepper Town or the Gas Plant neighborhood. Later, they would patrol their old haunts as police officers.

Leon Jackson played stickball on the streets. James King put skates on boxes and zoomed around the apron of a Gulf Oil service station on Ninth Street South. Freddie Lee Crawford and Baker started first grade together at the old Davis Academy on Third Avenue South.

Later, they went to Gibbs High School. They made the football team. Crawford was the center. Next to him on either side were guards Nero and King. Keys started at tackle, sometimes end. Baker played any position that was open. De Loach was a basketball player.

Crawford, remembered as a straight-A student, was by his own admission "brazen"—even in high school.

When the school system contracted with the city to send buses for Gibbs students, the buses had signs ordering "colored" to the rear. Crawford said he tore them down.

Gibbs was segregated then, as was virtually every other aspect of life in St. Petersburg.

"You couldn't even be caught downtown after dark unless you were walking to work," Jackson said.

It was the same elsewhere in Florida and in much of the South.

King said that when he was a child still living in the small community of Hernando in Citrus County, he saw men wearing striped clothes working on the roadside. He ran out of the house for a closer look. His mother called for him to come back. The men were prisoners, and King recalled a guard who yelled at his mother: "If you don't break him, we will."

King recalls his grandmother, Amanda King, who had been a slave. King remembers her as an elegant lady who always wore high-buttoned shoes, a long dress and a long-sleeved blouse buttoned to the neck. She told the story about her South Carolina owner selling her and her brother to a man in Florida. On the boat to St. Augustine, her brother was thrown overboard and drowned.

There was no such thing as ancient history. The past played a role in everyday life; it played into the decision black men made to become police officers.

Although a police job could mean a chance to make a difference in the Jim Crow system, officers often remained an unpleasant symbol.

"I had reservations initially," Nero said. He said he had seen how law enforcement could be used to suppress black people's rights.

"I didn't want to be seen in that light," he said.

Still, Nero and the others understood the implications of standing up to the city. Goliath Davis, a former police chief who became St. Petersburg's deputy mayor, said Crawford was especially farsighted.

"He had a keen sense of how pervasive law enforcement was, and is, in the life of folks. He knew that people of color had to be in policymaking decisions," said Davis, who joined the police department in 1974.

During the precarious '60s, Crawford's argument helped persuade his friends.

One or two at a time, the hometown kids applied. They passed civil service exams. They endured investigations, sometimes conducted secretly.

King worked at the Tramor Cafeteria downtown. One day he experienced a particularly exasperating customer.

"The guy would drop a fork and say, 'Go get me another fork, boy.' Then he'd deliberately drop the new one and tell me to go get another one," King said.

The customer turned out to be a police officer poking at a potential recruit's reaction, King said. King didn't get mad or rattled, which evidently meant he passed the "test."

The officers originally wanted to avoid a court fight. They met with police brass, hoping to make changes that would let them grow professionally. But nothing happened.

"We did not experience extensive racism in the ranks from the other officers," Nero said. "There was no in-your-face attitude displayed to us. Up the supervisory chain, this was where things got a little sticky."

Off-duty bull sessions kept the issues alive. Then a catalyst emerged.

Charlotte McCoy owned Doctors Pharmacy at 1421 Twenty-second Street South. It had a lunch counter and it was natural for the beat cops to stop in. Dr. Robert J. Swain had founded the pharmacy during the mid-1950s, establishing it in the business and apartment complex owned by Dr. Ralph Wimbish.

There, over sandwiches and midday banter, some of the officers met James B. Sanderlin, whose offices were two doors down. The lawyer already had

Judge James B. Sanderlin, the county's first African American judge, campaigned for civil rights as a young lawyer. *Courtesy of* The Weekly Challenger.

gone to court in 1964 seeking to desegregate county schools, a suit that would take seven years to resolve. Now he listened to what the cops had to say.

On May 11, 1965, Sanderlin filed a federal court suit. It charged the city with discrimination and demanded that it end. To pay the legal costs, the officers, most of whom earned a little more than two hundred dollars biweekly, took out a bank loan.

"It was done for ourselves to alleviate our pain," Baker said.

Sanderlin, who grew up in Petersburg, Virginia, and Washington, D.C., graduated from Howard University. He earned a law degree from Boston University and could have lived comfortably in the metropolitan Northeast.

But Sanderlin wanted to fight for civil rights. So the young lawyer moved to St. Petersburg when he was thirty-one. With Frank Peterman Sr. and Frank White, he opened an office on Twenty-second Street South.

Then the most important thoroughfare for the city's African American residents, a ten-block strip of Twenty-second Street brimmed with businesses, professional offices, grocery stores, a movie theater, a hotel, funeral homes, a hospital and bars and nightclubs.

On weekend nights, the bars and clubs boomed. Sometimes things got rough. Black officers might walk four abreast on the sidewalks to discourage trouble. To the northeast lay the three other black neighborhoods—Gas Plant, Methodist Town and the remnants of St. Petersburg's first black settlement, Pepper Town. They were part of what was referred to as zone thirteen. Within it, Twenty-second Street was called beat seven.

Zone thirteen was the only section black officers could patrol. No white officers could do so, according to court records at the time of the suit, although they eventually did so.

Black officers rarely got weekends off because supervisors said that was when they were most needed.

To Baker, it represented an unspoken white fear about "the black problem."

"I arrived at the conclusion I was being used," Baker said. "I thought about my situation. I was being used to handle the black problem. Our whole police policy was to have black policemen police black people."

Police brass didn't get that specific in public. But in its defense, the city denied discrimination, saying black officers were assigned to mostly black neighborhoods because they could do a better job there than white officers.

"Italian policemen would do better in Italian neighborhoods, too," a high-ranking officer was quoted as saying.

A newspaper called the suit "probably" the first of its kind in the nation under the 1964 Civil Rights Act.

The first round ended badly for the officers. Federal district Judge Joseph Lieb dismissed the case in March 1966. But Sanderlin appealed and, offering to pay the cost, the NAACP stepped in.

Leroy Clark, a lawyer for the NAACP's Legal Defense and Educational Fund, helped handle the appeal. It wasn't as though the NAACP had nothing else to do.

"It was astounding" how many cases the organization was dealing with at the time, Clark said in a 2007 interview.

But St. Petersburg brought a special challenge. Part of the case was "unique" and "difficult," Clark said, because Harold Smith, the police chief, didn't treat the black officers as inferiors but simply contended that they could do the job better in black neighborhoods.

"The problem is, it was too simplistic an analysis," Clark said. "It's a stereotypical assumption and it doesn't in any precise way hold up."

Delays stalled the case. Paperwork got lost. Finally, on August 1, 1968, the word came down. The Fifth U.S. Circuit Court of Appeals said that presumed police efficiency must yield to constitutional rights.

The court spelled out its decision in terse legal terms: "Reversed and remanded."

Said the court: "Nothing...is intended to suggest that the Negro officers on the police force of St. Petersburg should be given preferential treatment.

"They deserve only what they seek—equality."

The black officers had won.

Harold Smith, the police chief, said at the time the decision came down that policy changes the officers wanted had been made before the appeals court ruling. The African American officers were assigned citywide.

"You could tell there was resentment," Keys said, "but attitudes improved gradually."

Seven of the twelve who sued were still alive in 2007. In their sixties and seventies, most had long since retired. Five live in St. Petersburg. Sanderlin, who died in 1990, became Pinellas County's first black judge.

The officers saw themselves as civil rights warriors who got lost in history. But on September 13, 2007, the City of St. Petersburg honored the officers at a special city hall reception and ceremony. They were hailed as "the courageous twelve."

"A beacon for the community," council member Earnest Williams called the former officers.

"One little acre we concentrated on, within the whole civil rights movement," Baker said.

"After the suit, it wasn't easy. But we had each other," he said. "We like to think we stood up. We had nerve enough, we had decency enough for the moment," Baker said.

Said Davis: "It had tremendous ramifications for the overall community. It meant people of color had an opportunity to participate and it enhanced justice for everybody, not just a few."

Cedric Gordon, the assistant chief, put it this way: "We stood on their shoulders."

Chapter 7

The Power of the Word

*It is God's will that by doing right you should put to silence the
ignorance of foolish men.*

—One Peter 2:15

In November 1925 a shy, gangly young man arrived in St. Petersburg,
fresh from a Burke County, Georgia, farm. He did what many new
arrivals did. He went to work for Georgia Engineering Company and
earned twenty-one dollars a week installing the company's famous
Augusta blocks in Allendale and Rio Vista subdivisions and on Ninth
Street. On weekends, he found fun on a growing Twenty-second Street
South and he earned a reputation for hitting home runs at a Seventh
Avenue South baseball field.[56]

But Enoch Douglas Davis soon dedicated his life to the church and to the
struggle for African American equality. By the time he died in 1985, Davis
had been pastor of Bethel Community Baptist church for fifty-two years.
He championed the civil rights movement in St. Petersburg and has been
credited with defusing much of the tension that nearly plunged the city into
racial strife during the volatile sanitation strikes of 1968. It would not be an
exaggeration to say he became St. Petersburg's man for all seasons.

"Because of Enoch Davis' courage and voice of moderation, St. Petersburg
was spared the bloodshed and violence that erupted in other Florida cities
and across this nation during the height of the Civil Rights struggle in the
late '50s and early '60s," wrote A. Leon Lowry Sr., pastor of Beulah Baptist
Institutional Church in Tampa.

Don Jones, who served as St. Petersburg's mayor during part of the
turbulent 1960s, wrote this: "Enoch Davis never raised his voice, he never
pounded his fist. He simply reflected to the highest his love of God, his fellow
man, black or white, and his total community."

The Reverend Enoch Davis, considered a hero of St. Petersburg for his role in advancing civil rights while defusing violence, was pastor at Bethel Community Baptist Church for fifty-two years. *Courtesy of Hazel Barnes.*

Davis helped keep the city from coming apart. He served as a bridge between segregated black and white communities, often using his influence to help the younger members of the community. In 1958, he was the featured speaker at a meeting of the Children's Interracial Organization, held at the white Christ Methodist Church on First Avenue North downtown.

Just as importantly, his ministry at Bethel Community epitomized the importance of churches in the African American community. From stately temples with membership in the hundreds to storefront sanctuaries attended by ten or a dozen people, churches supplied the bonds that strengthened a black community separated from the mainstream culture.

The church's first mission always has been worship and spiritual comfort. But as authors C. Eric Lincoln and Lawrence H. Mamiya demonstrate in their in-depth work, *The Black Church in the African American Experience*, the churches provided a stable and empowering social experience more than any other institution.

Churches helped newcomers find homes and jobs. They fed and clothed the poor when other agencies would not. They combined their influence in speaking to the white establishment downtown.

They offered social opportunity as well. A sampling from the 1958 "Negro news pages" of the *St. Petersburg Times* suggests a multitude of activities:

The Southern Echoes, a gospel group, sang at the Church of the Faithful at Twelfth Street South and Elmore Avenue. The Gospel Chorus members of Travelers Rest Baptist Church put on a coffee as their chief St. Patrick's Day celebration. An "electrical wedding"—mock nuptials conducted to see which couples could produce the fanciest ceremony—took place at New

Hope Missionary Baptist. Lily White Lodge Number Forty-four held a baby popularity contest at the Fifth Avenue Community Chapel. St. Petersburg Ushers Circle Number One held its March literary and musical program at Mount Zion Progressive Baptist.[57]

Because both father and mother worked in many families, caring for the community's young people became another paramount church role. At the forefront was Happy Workers Day Nursery. If there is an institution as symbolic as Gibbs High School to African Americans, it might well be the nursery at 920 Nineteenth Street South.

Often credited with being the oldest social service agency in St. Petersburg, the center opened in 1929. It was founded in conjunction with Trinity Presbyterian Church by its pastor, the Reverend Oscar McAdams, and his wife, Willie Lee McAdams.

"It was the class of what was available for young black kids in those early days," said Don McRae, who was chief of staff for David Fischer, St. Petersburg's mayor during the 1990s. During the 1930s, McRae attended the day care center, which has served as many as six generations of the same family.

The Reverend McAdams, who spoke five languages and taught mathematics at Sixteenth Street Junior High School and Gibbs High School, in addition to Latin at Gibbs, started the church at the direction of the synod of Atlanta. It served what was then a relatively new but growing African American neighborhood, virtually in the country, webbed with dirt roads and often lighted only by kerosene lanterns on living room tables

Willie Lee McAdams was the force behind the nursery, which for years was known as "the McAdams center" or "Mrs. McAdams's place."

"She was just a towering figure kids looked up to. Her demeanor was one of wanting to give, not one of a disciplinarian," McRae said.

Five children, whose parents paid twenty-five cents a week, composed the first kindergarten. At the urging of Lillian Ramsey, infant care began at the center in 1943, with parents paying two dollars a week if they could afford it.

The Children's Interracial Organization was created the same year to support the nursery and kindergarten. One of the group's missions was to raise funds and, in 1966, it put on a benefit featuring Coretta Scott King, the widow of Dr. Martin Luther King Jr. The program, billed as a freedom concert, was held at Pasadena Community Church, a well-established and influential white church.

The center was designated a city historic site in 1998.[58]

Through the years, every one of the seven major black denominations, as outlined by Lincoln and Mamiya, has had a presence in St. Petersburg. They include the African Methodist Episcopal Church; the African Methodist Episcopal Zion Church; the Christian Methodist Episcopal Church; the National Baptist Convention, U.S.A.; the National Baptist Convention of America, Unincorporated; the Progressive National Baptist Convention; and the Church of God in Christ.

It is not certain when or where the first African American place of worship was situated. Perhaps it was in a home or small store in Pepper Town, the first black settlement. Pepper Town had by 1912 at least one church, Mount Temor Baptist at Second Avenue South and Eighth Street, but no record suggests it was the first.

By 1920, seven major congregations were meeting, as were several smaller fellowships.[59] In 1951, a few years before the civil rights movement hit its peak in St. Petersburg, there were more than forty black churches listed in the Polk City directory for that year.

Certainly among the pioneer churches, and the one that gave Methodist Town its name, was Bethel African Methodist Episcopal. It was established near what became Third Avenue North and Tenth Street.

Bethel AME was first built in 1894, and the Methodist Town neighborhood grew up around it. The Reverend J.S. Braswell was the pastor. Built of wood originally, a larger masonry church known as the "Stone Church" was built across the street in 1905.

Work started in 1922 on the current building, which was modeled after the denomination's mother church, Bethel AME in Philadelphia. The St. Petersburg church was built over the footprint of the old church and, according to records, just one Sunday service had to be interrupted because of construction.

Among the founders were local businessmen or laborers who worked or donated construction material to help build the original church and its subsequent buildings. They included Charles Hargrave, property owner; Ancell McLaughlin, insurance agent; Loomis Williams, land developer; Jake Hughes, hotelier and landowner; Nathaniel Williams, mortician; Robert Blue, grocery store proprietor; and Albert Debose, developer.[60]

Lena Reynolds began attending the Tenth Street Church of God in Methodist Town in 1910, two years after she came to St. Petersburg.

Years later, she remembered when the church building was moved to 207 Tenth Street North. The congregation had purchased the First Presbyterian Church building from the white part of town.

"Oh, they were happy when that church turned the corner," Reynolds told a writer in 1979. "My class at Sunday school had the blocks all ready to set the building on."

She recalled the church's first pastor as A.J. Simmons, who built a twelve- by twenty-four-foot structure for the original congregation. When the new building arrived, it had dark green gingerbread trim to go with the white coat of paint. The congregation soon painted the entire church white, and in 2007, the building looked much the same as it did nearly a century earlier. It is one of the few remaining buildings of old Methodist Town, Bethel AME being another.[61]

Reverend Joseph E. Walton was another of the church's early pastors. He stayed for several years. There were several pastors in between his tenure and when his wife Lilla became pastor in 1951 and served in that capacity to 1956. They were from "up north," according to Elaine Jenkins.

"She was a sweet lady; very warmhearted, with snow-white hair and always beat a drum before offering her sermon," said Jenkins, who was about ten years old at the time and vividly recalls lively services led by Reverend Lilla Simmons. Jenkins recalls that during those days, the church was packed, with hardly an empty seat, Sunday after Sunday.[62]

Another early Methodist Town church was Mount Olive Primitive Baptist on Tenth Street North, established in 1915. Its two rooms held about fifty people. A kitchen took up most of a small third room. A plain wooden cross about four feet high stood behind the pulpit and people sat on benches facing it.

An early member was Mathews Coley, a boxer who trained near the church and later operated a shoeshine stand on the west side of Ninth Street North. He recalled in 1977 that an early pastor was Oliver B. Bartley.

King Tolliver was a deacon in the Tenth Street Church of God in Methodist Town. He and his wife Fannie were widely known for their natty style of dress. *Courtesy of* The Weekly Challenger.

The same year, Coley told a writer about a 1925 New Year's celebration, the biggest he could remember. The church meeting started at about 7:00 p.m. and lasted until the next morning.

Coley recalled:

> *They had a big eat. Now, New Year's night they served everybody on long tables. They didn't have lights like we do now, but we had lamps and lanterns strung up over the tables and where we had the meeting. It was the gladdest. It was a good time. And the old sisters came out with their long dresses. Oh, it was a lovely world then.*[63]

Lillie Mae Peterson, Bartley's daughter, also recalled the all-night watches. She said her father sometimes didn't start preaching until 4:00 a.m., but people would stay through the preliminaries to hear the sermon. She also recalled baptismal ceremonies in which members would dress in white and parade from the church to Tampa Bay for the immersion.

A baptism takes place on the South Mole beach, which became the modern Demens Landing park. The participants in this ceremony could not be identified. *Courtesy of* The Weekly Challenger.

Also striking were the foot washing ceremonies, held the first Sunday of every month. "The church would be packed with just as many white people as colored," Peterson said.

Mount Olive was torn down in 1977 as urban renewal came to Methodist Town.

One church was of unusual design and deserved to be saved on its historic merit alone. First Institutional Baptist Church in the Gas Plant neighborhood was called the "Shell Dash" church because it was built with seashells. It was razed when Tropicana Field and its parking lot were built.

Like Davis, other clergyman used their influence to crusade for civil rights. One of them was the Reverend John Wesley Carter, pastor of Bethel Metropolitan Baptist Church. Carter also served as president of the local NAACP chapter.

Davis called Carter "easily one of the greatest preachers who ever pastored a church in St. Petersburg." He said that Carter had "less than one-eighth" African blood, and because of his light complexion, "could have gone to any hotel, motel or restaurant in the downtown area of our city and would have been accorded the same courtesy that any white man received, but he chose not to enjoy these privileges while his black constituency could not enjoy them."[64]

Davis was consistently in the forefront of St. Petersburg's freedom movement. With Chester James, J.P. Moses and Dr. Fred Alsup, Davis helped organize the Citizens Cooperative Committee in 1952. He appeared several times before the city council, asking for better job opportunities and equal pay for equal work. Threats of injury and even death did not deter him, and city police, as well as his Masonic brothers, patrolled the pastor's home at all hours to keep him safe.[65]

Police respected him so much that white officers sometimes brought black offenders to him rather than to jail.

When the Freedom Riders aboard segregated buses visited St. Petersburg in 1961, Davis arranged for them to be met at the bus station downtown and taken to Bethel Community Baptist. Police officers escorted—or kept an eye on—the Freedom Riders whenever they left the church. Often the excursions were to Davis's home or that of Ralph and Bette Wimbish, where they were able to relax. There were no unsavory incidents during the Freedom Riders' short stay in St. Petersburg.

Davis died on September 29, 1985, at age seventy-seven. He had retired from the Bethel Community pastorate after fifty-two years, often credited as being the longest pastoral tenure in city history. During his service he was given the Liberty Bell Award by the St. Petersburg Bar Association for his

Bethel Metropolitan Baptist Church stood at 301 Tenth Street South in the Gas Plant
neighborhood. *Courtesy of the City of St. Petersburg.*

calming influence during the sanitation workers' strike. The city named a
$1.6 million civic center after him in 1981. He ran unsuccessfully for the city
council in 1969.

"I wonder," wrote *St. Petersburg Times* columnist Peggy Peterman, "If St.
Petersburg can produce any more such heroes."

Chapter 8

How Much Remains?

Do what we do.

—*Tony Dungy*

Pepper Town is gone.

Methodist Town is gone, except for its old churches.

The Gas Plant neighborhoods are gone, replaced by Tropicana Field and its sprawling parking lot.

Much of the Twenty-second Street South community is gone, although the city government in the early twenty-first century continues to work hard to rehabilitate the once thriving corridor.

The redevelopment in those neighborhoods changed the appearance of St. Petersburg and the lives of the people who lived in them.

In many cases, former residents were able to move into better housing. Some suggest that their old neighborhoods had tumbled into the abyss of illegal drugs and the crime that comes with them, and that change was for the better.

At the same time, the change disrupted the continuity of people's lives. Gas Plant redevelopment caused 285 buildings to be bulldozed; more than 500 households and 9 churches had to be relocated; and more than 30 businesses moved or closed.[66]

Tenements and shacks disappeared, but so did the fine homes in places like Sugar Hill, where the elegant Ponder home and its beloved cherry hedge disappeared, as did a score of other well-appointed houses. Even people who lived in less pleasant circumstances felt the sting of displacement—what some call a slum or a shack may be no less a home and a roof overhead to a family, a grandmother or a single mother.

Along with the construction of Interstate 275 and the displacement it caused, probably no other project caused the degree of resentment that the

These unidentified youngsters at Jordan Elementary School learn what it means to vote during a civics lesson in the 1950s. *Courtesy of Norman Jones II.*

Gas Plant bulldozing did. Part of it was because residents there had believed renewal of another kind was coming, a baseball stadium. The decision was not universally popular because baseball had not been part of the original plan. The original plan to rehabilitate the Gas Plant neighborhood called for new housing, an industrial park and hundreds of new jobs.

When the idea of baseball came up, city council member David Welch warned officials:

> *When you went into this area and moved out all the people, you said you were going to rehabilitate and create light industry and create jobs. You have a moral obligation to those individuals who were moved out for what you have told them.*[67]

The other neighborhoods experienced upheaval of equal magnitude. To be sure, not all the effects were negative, but among them were the disappearance of a sense of place and the pervasive bonding within a community—the loss of connectivity. The late *St. Petersburg Times* columnist

The Gas Plant area experienced some new construction in the 1960s, but all of it disappeared when a baseball stadium was built. One of the huge storage cylinders that gave the neighborhood its name is visible in the background. *Courtesy of the City of St. Petersburg.*

Peggy Peterman always lamented that the young people lost the most when they were deprived of constant contact with their elders, which had been so much a part of the lives of people who had grown up in an earlier era.

As city council member Rene Flowers observed during a 2007 public meeting, "People in the community found money to educate young people, and send them to college."

Still, people have moved on with their lives. As coauthor Rosalie Peck suggests in an essay, carrying a grudge is counterproductive (see Epilogue).

"The greatest blessing of change is that racism no longer paralyzes the heart and soul of the city," wrote Peck, a lifelong resident who experienced, firsthand, segregation's malevolent ways.

Moreover, role models for young people remain. They work as hard as their forebears did generations ago. They think of a city's children. They try to make life better for the African American community, which more and more has become part of the citywide community. Many are unsung heroes, such as Wilma Green, who for several years operated a program called Agape, teaching girls how to succeed, and Constance Samuels, a pastor who took special care of troubled young people. She was a foster mother to literally hundreds of children for more than thirty years, taking into her home as many as eight or

Left: For years, the old South Mole beach was the only public swimming area in St. Petersburg for African Americans. The Million Dollar Pier, where blacks were not allowed, is visible in the background. *Courtesy of the City of St. Petersburg.*

Below: This photo, taken in the 1950s, looks south from the South Mole beach. Visible in the background is the coast guard station at Bayboro Harbor. *Courtesy of the City of St. Petersburg.*

nine young people at a time, some with felony records including murder and robbery. Juvenile authorities had given up on some of them.

In his inauguration speech upon assuming presidency of the local NAACP chapter, Darryl Rouson made this definitive (and lyrical) comment: "The black community is not a monody of monolithic thought expressed in monologue, but a multifaceted community made up of a mosaic of cultural talents and leaders."[68]

The Reverend Louis Murphy, pastor of Mount Zion Progressive Missionary Baptist Church comes to mind. A district Boy Scout executive before he became a pastor, Murphy helped encourage the city's scouting organizations, as did such individuals as James Hall, Elzie Williams and Delores Fletcher. Murphy also is consistently involved with community projects to end street violence.

Lounell Britt is the executive director of the James B. Sanderlin Family Center, overseeing a multitude of programs that offer life skills, legal advice, computer classes, spouse-abuse intervention, music classes, health information and education. All the services are free.

At age ninety-two, Mattie Gardner still recited poetry and oratory, reading to senior citizens at congregate dining sites. She did it all her life, while serving as a PTA leader throughout her children's careers at Davis Elementary, Sixteenth Street Junior High and Gibbs High School.

Her daughter, Teresena Bryant, described her mother as an activist. "My mother was the Fannie Lou Hamer and Rosa Parks of St. Petersburg," Bryant said, referring to civil rights icons. She continued:

> *I remember her leading the fight many times during my youth. In 1955 she was the leader of the maids' walk-out for better treatment and increase in wages at Mound Park Hospital. While we were at Sixteenth Street Junior High School, she led the fight to rescind the request that parents pay for towel services for gym, and won. Those are but a few of the instances where my mother willingly led the fight for equal rights and justice for all.*[69]

Mattie Lee Cooksey Gardner died in 2005 at age 103, when her activist roots were recalled. During the 1890s in Georgia, her father, Wise Child Solomon Cooksey, spoke out for African American equality as the tide began to turn back gains made during Reconstruction. Lascy Daniels, age 96, was Mrs. Gardner's friend for more than sixty years. She recalled that Mrs. Gardner could recite the whole of William Cullen Bryant's eighty-one-line "Thanatopsis," often considered the first major American poem.[70]

Norman Jones II is a student and curator who dedicated his life to researching African American history. Much of his efforts have focused on St. Petersburg and on his father's career. *Courtesy of Norman Jones II.*

Historians like Norman Jones II and Minson Rubin work diligently to preserve memories of their communities. Volunteers staff the Carter G. Woodson museum on Ninth Avenue South, a venue where young people can learn about history and take part in researching it.

City council members Earnest Williams and Rene Flowers, school board member Mary Brown, county commissioners Calvin Harris and Ken Welch—the latter a scion of the pioneer Welch family—and state legislator Frank Peterman Jr. are current role models who have used their leadership positions to influence young lives.

Among those who stand tallest in that realm is Vyrle Davis, who in 1960 began teaching at Sixteenth Street Junior High School when teachers were expected to raise twenty-five dollars to buy pupils basic supplies.

Davis retired in 1995 as an area superintendent, which is among the loftiest positions in the school district. During a career filled with achievements, Davis always said that he was proudest of things he was able to do to help youngsters. For example, he created Ebony Scholars and 500 Role Models for Excellence, organizations that recognize and encourage the achievements of young people.

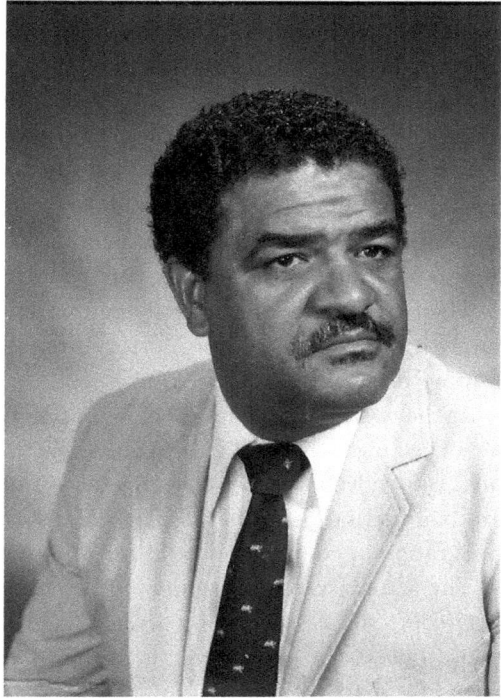

Vyrle Davis is a respected educator and community activist who founded organizations to encourage African American youngsters in school. *Courtesy of* The Weekly Challenger.

"He's done a lot of super things for the school system and for the community," said Bob Safransky, a former colleague. "He's done a lot to help make St. Petersburg a better place for everybody to live."[71]

Refusing to take up the easy chair upon his retirement, Davis also was the driving force behind two community activist organizations: the African American Voters Research and Education Committee in 1996 and, two years later, Concerned Organizations for Quality Education for Black Students. The former is credited with securing a 1999 referendum victory for single-member county commission districts, considered imperative for African American candidates running for election in largely black neighborhoods. The victory ensured that they could run in their neighborhoods rather than being required to campaign countywide.

The 1999 referendum campaign was a genuine grass-roots effort, drawing its life from several neighborhoods.

"I even yelled out my car window at people around Wildwood Park," said resident Mittie Pounds. "Vote! Today is vote!"

With a meager $300 budget, Doris Swangles and Inez McRae spearheaded a small task force to get out the vote. Swangles, a 1953 Gibbs High School graduate had some political experience, having worked on Jesse Jackson's presidential campaigns in 1988 and 1992. "There's a time when you've got to take a stand whether you win or lose. You've just got to get out there and let people know what you're about," Swangles said.

Facing opposition that included the powerful construction industry, Swangles and McRae led what came to be called "the nine-day blitz," making scores of telephone calls, handing out thousands of fliers at churches and in parking lots and making sure people got to the polls.

Their classic, street level campaign resulted in a twenty-three-vote victory, surely one of St. Petersburg history's significant moments as the twentieth century drew to a close.

As the twenty-first century begins to unfold, African American leaders face new challenges that will affect youngsters' lives. Among the more important ones is the idea of school choice, which at this writing school district officials are considering. It takes the place of court-ordered busing, which created integration in county schools starting in 1971.

The choice program under consideration could result in a dozen St. Petersburg schools becoming desegregated. There is a debate about whether that would be a good thing for African American pupils. While no one wants the bad, old days of Jim Crow to return, there is thought given to whether black youngsters might fare better scholastically in settings with predominantly black student populations. Yet many argue for the benefits of a diverse school environment.

Much of this book has dealt with the tribulations of segregation and the social fault lines caused when people are not exposed to, or have no understanding of the culture of others. At best, the alienation is limiting; at worst, it can be deadly. At the least, it is frustrating and frightening.

The experience of a couple who knew both segregation and integration is worthwhile to contemplate, and as it merges two worlds, it seems an appropriate way to close the main part of this book. Russell Allen and his wife Andrea Yvette Allen shared their story with coauthor Jon Wilson nearly a decade before this writing.

One of Russell Allen's worlds was the St. Petersburg of the early 1960s, when schools were strictly segregated. Allen began first grade, learning to read from books that, more often than not, were so old they were missing pages.

His second world was the one of integration's early days in St. Petersburg. Graduating from high school in 1975, Allen experienced the boiling tension that resulted when black and white students first shared classrooms in large numbers and struggled to get past an era not quite buried.

Allen uses words such as "devastating" to describe that time. But it was a learning experience, he said, and a time of growing.

The lessons weren't always easy.

Court-ordered busing for desegregation—a policy forged to dissolve once and for all Pinellas County's separate and unequal schools—sometimes brought confrontation. Black and white students had never come together before. How could they be expected to relate, let alone come to like one another?

There were cafeteria fights. Sometimes police came to keep order on campuses. Even students who tried to get along experienced hurt feelings and misunderstanding. Allen remembers being spat upon and called a racist name.

Andrea Yvette Allen never attended segregated schools and can only wonder at Russell's stories about integration's early turmoil on campus.

Still, she had been accustomed to a separate world, too. The trauma of her first day in school, when white children entered her life for the first time, remains vivid. It is sometimes the first story she relates about her school life.

"I sat at my desk and wet my pants because I was afraid," she said. "I just remember crying. I didn't want to ask to go. They couldn't get me out of my desk. It was all out of fear and not knowing" what to do in a racially mixed setting.

Part of her trepidation stemmed from the unusual attention she was paid. "When I went to class, [the white children] stared at me," she said. "They weren't used to me."

Her white teacher at Lakewood Elementary, whose name she doesn't remember, was kind.

"'Honey,' she said, 'Why didn't you tell me?'"

Her mother came to school that day and stayed every day for a month to reassure the first grader. "It took me a long time to get comfortable," Andrea Allen said.

Later, when she had her own children, she vowed the same thing wouldn't happen to them.

"I made sure they didn't go to anything predominantly black," she said, beginning with preschool. Even though some of their black friends wondered why, the Allens drove their four children from their apartment on Fifty-fourth Avenue South to a private school in the Tyrone area, perhaps a twenty-two-mile round trip.

"I want my children to be comfortable. I want my kids to grow up with white kids, black kids, Hispanic kids," Andrea Allen said, "so they don't have to go through what I did, so they won't have a complex."

Some African American parents remain concerned that schools south of Central Avenue in St. Petersburg might revert to second-class status when it comes to supplies and official attention. In 1998, the Allens were already worried.

"Down there," Andrea Allen said then. "That's what people call where we live, 'down there,' instead of south St. Petersburg. We're going to become 'down there' if that plan is passed."

It is not just making sure there are enough books and that the air conditioning works. The Allens worried then, and parents continue to worry in 2007, about what will become of magnet programs and fundamental schools. (Magnet schools use special programs—for example, a focus on arts, international studies or science—to desegregate schools voluntarily. Fundamental schools rely on highly structured programs to attract students.)

Avyon, the Allens' oldest daughter, attended the medical magnet program at Boca Ciega. The other three children attended the Perkins Elementary magnet school for arts and international studies.

And beyond the concern about school quality, they wonder if something won't be lost if it should develop that fewer people of different races come together.

"The sooner white and black come together, the sooner you come to communication," said Russell Allen, who as a real estate agent has enjoyed a clientele divided equally between black and white. "Our kids came to it from day one. They don't see color."

Allen did see it when he went to school, and so did his classmates. In 1971, he went to Sixteenth Street Junior High (the middle school designation came later), and then to Pinellas Park Junior High in 1972. In 1975, he graduated from Boca Ciega High School, where he was vice-president of the black culture club.

A degree of integration had begun even before the federal busing order in 1971. Even in small doses, the changes brought tension. It was while walking home from Sixteenth Street that, Russell Allen said, he was spat upon.

"I'll tell you something. I was hurt, and I was angry. But you know, it goes back to what my father taught me. There're good whites and bad whites, good blacks and bad blacks. In the '60s, you dealt with that firsthand."

At Pinellas Park, Allen recalled, he was trying to eat a lunch of spaghetti and meatballs when silverware, milk cartons and food started flying in the cafeteria. A fight had broken out between black and white students. Later, at Boca Ciega, there were more battles. He said he had conversations with veteran Pinellas educator Hugh Kriever, then the principal, about why the youngsters were fighting one another.

The situation "was devastating. We [had] never sat side by side with white kids," he said. He continued:

> *Let's face it. Your hair's different, your skin's different. Black kids didn't listen to white kids' music, white kids didn't listen to ours. It was a learning experience. We found out we had things in common. We got a soul, we have emotions, we have feelings.*

Allen said he had few confrontations, crediting much of that good fortune to his father's influence. Besides, he said, "A man who runs to violence is a man who has run out of ideas."

Andrea Allen had a smoother path. After she adjusted to first grade, her school career took off. She played clarinet and flute. She had white friends. She walked to the home of one of them for Girl Scouts.

Her experiences with classmates and teachers were positive. "We weren't told we couldn't do this or that. The white kids didn't treat us any different," she said, whether at Lakewood or Bay Vista elementary schools, Bay Point Junior High or Lakewood High School, from which she graduated in 1981.

She and her brother Leroy Williams, a year older, actually had more confrontations with black youngsters who started later in predominantly white schools and couldn't understand how the sister and brother were able to get along with white classmates.

It wasn't until she graduated from the University of South Florida and started working that she began to encounter racism.

"Going into the working world was an eye-opener for me," said Andrea Allen, a state probation officer. She said she would hear co-workers talking about her getting the job only because she was a black woman and because of affirmative action.

"My father had to sit me down and say, hey, this is reality," she said.

Andrea Allen doesn't believe the best interests of youngsters lie in segregated schools. "I'm not calling it a black issue," she said in 1998. "I'm calling it a children's issue."

She likes to think of her Angelique and what she said when she was eight years old while wondering about being referred to as black.

"I'm not black, I'm brown," said Angelique, holding up crayons of the colors.

Andrea said: "I told her, 'Well, you see white people aren't like the white crayon, either.'"

Angelique responded: "I don't know who made these names up. Someone else should have done it."

But Where Did All the Mangoes Go?

As this book became reality, cherished memories of some of the "best years of our lives" emerged. Pleasant recollections of people, places, situations and times surfaced without exception during every interview or casual conversation, relative to the writing of what we have added to "the rest of the story" about African American community, culture and connectivity.

It has been fascinating to tell the story of and about more people, more historical events and long awaited social changes today visible in St. Petersburg, this Southern city so beautifully blessed by nature, but once besieged and marred by hateful, segregationist, racist control.

Yet in interview after interview came effortless expressions of cherished memories: memories of carefree, childhood days of undisturbed moments of peace as well as recollections of painful, troubled times.

Barbra Streisand sings, "What's too painful to remember, we simply choose to forget." But in this case, in terms of troubled yesteryears, overcoming and moving on was paramount and bearing grudges was never an issue. So it was no surprise to hear words and encouraging tones of optimism laced with expressed hope for continuing progress riding on the winds of change.

Blessed be the older generations, the children and grandchildren of slaves. Blessed be the spirit of the never-to-be-forgotten pioneers, who through perseverance, prayer, determination, suffering and endurance, like their ancestors never gave up the dream and promise of a brighter day. Blessed be those early black settlers, who while building the city and struggling to survive never relinquished belief and a liberating hold on the everlasting anchors of faith in God, in justice and in the hope of promised winds of change that they knew, deep in the marrow of their bones, were bound to come.

One of the pleasantries of writing the rest of the story was the experience of hearing more historical accounts. Almost without exception people of all ages recalled the recent, wretched, raw, race-based years before the advent of civil rights, which finally brought relief and easier times to long-suffering black citizens. The memories were both painful and pleasant, and most interviews were not unlike friendly front porch gatherings of old.

Someone invariably asked: "But where did all the mangoes go?"

The question came from those who remember times when no matter what was—or was not—in the ice box, on the supper table or on the grocery list, there was something to eat outside.

It was a time when "south side" children romped through sandspurs, palmettos and pine trees, enjoying access to an endless abundance of hunger-chasing, gut-filling, taste bud–satisfying fruit from trees of unlimited kindness.

Everywhere were wonderful fruit-bearing trees that seemed to belong to no one and to everyone. Merciful shade-bearing trees sagged heavy with guavas, avocadoes, oranges, grapefruit, tangerines and lemons always present for the picking.

"I knew where all the best mango trees were," Nadine Henderson laughed. "The turpentines were stringy. Ladyfingers were tasty. But my favorites were the pineapples. They were the best of all." Nadine's secret favorite mango tree location was probably shared by every child of the community, but one could hear in her voice the glee of recollection.

Mangoes were not the only hunger-chasing trees of plenty available to one and all. Along Sixteenth Street, from the site of the latter-day John Hopkins Middle School to the corner of Ninth Avenue South, a sprawling Gill Dairy Farm stood framed by some of the city's best avocado trees. Huge avocadoes fell to the ground and were readily available to any passerby.

Like the mango, avocado trees graced yards of many private homes and open fields throughout the south side community. Guavas, like mangoes, also were plentiful in a variety of flavors. White meat, yellow meat and pink meat described the delicate, succulent seed-filled fruit. They were the source of delicious homemade jam and jelly in many homes.

Many nurturing trees towered fifty feet tall in open fields, tempting fearless boys and girls—and young men and women—to climb the heights for choice rewards. Bushy guava trees were less of a challenge and more plentiful in backyards than woods, and more easily accessible.

Sparkling Tampa Bay offered shiners, sheepshead, grouper, red snapper, crabs and other sea life, which—like the fruit trees—was important to survival, especially during the Great Depression when work was scarce or often nonexistent.

But of all the readily accessible food sources of nature, mangoes are the most affectionately remembered. I noted at some point the longstanding absence of the once plentiful trees, particularly because growing up I enjoyed the crème de la crème of mangoes. Years later during an unforgettable stay in Haiti, I was awed by the size, color and majestic splendor of the exotic fruit hanging in profusion and royal grandeur in magnificent canopies of indescribable beauty. By day, they offered surreal displays of oval, succulent goodness in mixed, vibrant colors of red, yellow, orange, purple and gold, enhanced by the light of day. In the middle of the night, falling fruit ceremoniously thumped the earth like drumbeats.

Mango trees still can be spotted here and there in St. Petersburg, but the abundant harvest, once so readily available, is gone. Old-timers with cherished childhood memories wonder why.

Remember the big freeze of 1961 right around Christmastime? Remember when orange groves and woods, and almost every other thing green turned brown as if ravaged by fire? That's when the mangoes died, I believe—and guavas, oranges, lemons, tangerines and mulberries, too.

When is the last time you saw a guava? There was a time when guavas, like mangoes, were plentiful in a variety of flavors. You could find them in fields and the backyards of generous neighbors, friends and strangers. But all of that has changed. Gone are open fields. And backyards are becoming scarce.

As Forrest Gump might have said in his simplistic, but profound manner of speaking, "Things change." They do and they have. The greatest blessing of change is that racism no longer paralyzes the heart and soul of St. Petersburg, Florida. And in recent years, the major hub of the city, downtown St. Petersburg, has been resurrected. It embraces a cultural and physical renaissance of gargantuan proportions. Part of south St. Petersburg, historically defined as the major residential area for most of the city's black residents, in 2007 is officially known as Midtown, with many improvements and necessary amenities present. It continues to be a work in progress.

And while the consensus of the people is that "we've come a long way baby, but we still have a long way to go," the good news in view of undeniable progress is that there is still room for hope.

Almost always during interviews for this book, opportunity for nostalgic trips down memory lane prompted expressions of pride and pain interfaced with joy and pleasure. Heartfelt, sometimes simplistic yet poignant stories support truth, healing, insight, strength and beauty within contexts that validate historical events as experienced by St. Petersburg's earliest black pioneers and those who came later. Today's black citizenry is not, nor would their ancestors be, awed or mystified by substantial changes for opportunities, progress and possibilities made available.

Nor would they be mystified by the improved climate of humanity and human decency. They, as did their ancestors from Africa who survived slavery's harsh winters, have always known that a bright day of freedom would come. The legacy is steeped in the tradition of endurance, sacrifice and the will to overcome hardships of gargantuan proportions matched only by unequaled determination to survive and build a better future for their children.

Positive role models of old were recalled as being as plentiful as fruit-bearing trees. Revered in memory are parents, relatives, principals, teachers, coaches, preachers, friends, neighbors, professionals in multiple fields and ordinary people doing extraordinary things. Changes that made things better inevitably altered a highly valued built-in system of protective and personal interaction—the support that developed out of need.

But the legacy of courageous leadership lives on. "Do not go where the path may lead; go instead where there is no path and leave a trail," was a lesson well learned. Those words of Ralph Waldo Emerson speak to the continuum of strength, vision and tenacity willed to younger generations. Many grasped the mantle of ambition, responsibility and pride. They continue to make a difference in the lives of countless children, in society, in the city and indeed in the world.

St. Petersburg today is nearly bereft of mangoes and other cherished fruits of trees from neighborhood yards, but the city is still wealthy with a continuing supply of the soul-sustaining fruit of the human spirit.

Rosalie Peck

Heroes of World War II

Where is Pearl Harbor?
Those were the first words spoken in almost every household in St. Petersburg when news came over the radio that the Japanese had bombed the naval base in Hawaii.

Even after its geography was nervously determined by neighborly word of mouth, and by consulting encyclopedias for more information, Pearl Harbor to most Floridians still seemed light-years away, temporarily easing fears of children and parents, but warning all, on that balmy, sunny, winter afternoon, that the world was in danger.

War would follow. The dreadful thought was a foregone conclusion even for children too young to know or to comprehend the terrible ramifications of the term. But soon after the infamous attack on Pearl Harbor on that quiet morning of December 7, 1941, every household of every neighborhood of the city would be affected, to various degrees, by sacrifice and pain.

From the most distant black neighborhoods of the city in the far southeast district that surrounded Gibbs High School—in the "country," as the palmetto- and pine-lined area was called—to the "privileged" dusty, unpaved roads, alleys and avenues of the electric-lighted community of Methodist Town, black teenage boys and full-grown men would soon be called to serve—full measure, skin color notwithstanding—the country that for years before and thereafter denied their civil rights.

One by one they were drafted, called to arms as men duty-bound to serve. Loyal in peace and strife, they went to war. Some never returned. All who did found immediately upon their return that nothing had changed.

The 1944 foreword to the Gibbs High School yearbook contained these words:

*We want to remember faces which we shall probably never see again, for
at this very moment a terrible war is raging throughout the earth, and in
a few weeks some of us who pen this book will be in the conflict fighting
for the freedoms that make lives worth living!*

Editor in chief Albert Allen, a brilliant senior student, wrote the poignant
commentary.

The Gibbs High School class of 1947 dedicated its yearbook to the
veterans who were—or had been—among their schoolmates. Many former
students returned to school after having traveled throughout the world,
exchanging guns for the greater weapons of books and pens. After the war,
some went on to become proficient in industrial training, woodwork, shoe
repair, barbering, manual arts, tailoring and designing, auto mechanics and
mechanical drawing at Gibbs High School. Using the GI Bill, others went on
to college and postgraduate degrees.

On the home front at Gibbs, teachers Eloise Perkins and O.B. McLin
organized the Woman's Army for National Defense (WAND). It enabled girls
of all ages to aid the war effort in nonmilitary ways. Girls too young to join
the Women's Army Corps (WAC) eagerly became members of WAND, an
organization designed to be active in peace as well as in war.

Initial officers at Gibbs High School were: Verdya Dennard, captain;
Rosalie Peck and Laura Allen, first and second lieutenants, respectively;
Pauline Ruth Givens, master sergeant; Gladys Allen, sergeant; Eunice Cason,
first Sergeant; and Annie Lee Minton, chaplain. Numerous students enrolled
as cadets during the first year. The purpose of WAND was to help the war
effort. The organization did its part to help soldiers far from home find
friends and affiliations within the community during their tours of duty in
the city. They introduced them to families, encouraged them and exchanged
mail when they moved on to distant, dangerous assignments. They also
helped them to choose a church in which to worship, and sold war bonds
and stamps.

A major highlight and moment of great pride took place on March 10,
1945, when WAND members escorted Dr. Mary McLeod Bethune, president
of Bethune-Cookman College of Daytona Beach, Florida, to the podium of
the Gibbs auditorium, where she praised WAND's efforts and announced
that the inspector general of the United States would be visiting the campus
in the spring.

Several young women served in the active military. Among them were
Andrian Lee, Theo Peck, Gwendolyn Shelby and Eliza Williams-Daniels.

Theo Peck was one of several female graduates of Gibbs High School who served in the military during World War II. *From the private collection of Rosalie Peck.*

Gibbs High School teacher and legendary jazz musician Alvin Downing served with the famed Tuskegee Airmen. Shown as a lieutenant here, Downing reached the rank of major. *Courtesy of* The Weekly Challenger.

Clarence Edward "Shad" Williams, among St. Petersburg's first black Eagle Scouts, was a United States Marine in World War II. *From the private collection of Rosalie Peck.*

Heroes of World War II

Among teachers who served were Alvin Downing, Julius Bradley, Albert Brooks, Julius K. Neal, Walter A. Armwood, Theodore Johnson, Louis D. Brown Sr., Noah B. Gaines and Alonzo Stephens.

Below is a partial list of Gibbs graduates and students who served in World War II:

Alexander Abrams II
Joseph Abrams
Calvin Adams
John Henry Barrance
Oliver Bartley
Eddie Battles
Torrence Benjamin
Roosevelt Bennett
Freddie Bostick
James Boyd
Clarence Bradley
J.L. Bradley
J.D. Brown
William Brown
Issac Bryant
Marion Bryant
Jessie Buoy
Lois Burnette
Eddie Bush
Charles Campbell
Burley Carter
George Childs
John Jacob Childs
Edward Clark
Frank Collins
Roosevelt Culver
Nathaniel Currington
Eddie Dallas
Solomon Dancil
Cecil Dandy

Henry Dandy
Alphonso Daniels
Valucius Dorsey
Willie Doyle II
Freddie Drayton
Adolphus Everette
Clinton Falana
Ernest Fillyau
William Fuller
George Gamble
Andrew Gilbert
Frank Gilmore
Eugene Givens
Lorenzo Graham
Willie Green
Althea Harris
James Harris
Jerome Harris
John Edward Harris
Jesse Henderson
Robert Henry
Leroy Huff
James J. Jackson
Chester James
Ralph James
Timothy Johnson
Althea Jones
James Keys
Napoleon Kicklighter
Robert Kidd
George King
James Knowles
Cyrus Latson
Joseph Lovett
Willie Lovett
Isadore Maeo
B.H. Martin

Eddie Martin
Arnold Matthews
Henry Matthews
Eugene McCoy
James R. McCoy
Grant McCray
Joseph McDaniel
Samuel McGarrah
Alex McLin
Daniel McNeil
Willie Minton
Edward Moody
Prince Moon
Alphonso Muldrew
Isaiah Porter
John Howard Quarles
Ausley Reed
Calvin Reed
J.C. Reed
James Riley
Benjamin Robinson
C.J. Robinson
Samuel Robinson
Johnnie Rogers
Simon Scott
William Scott
Douglas Seay
Earl Seay
Earl Seay Jr.
Johnny Seay
Rudolph Seay
Rufus Seay
Willie Seay Sr.
Thomas Simmons
Wilbur Simmons
Charles Smith
Isaiah Smith
J.B. Smith II
Richard Smith

Robert Smith
William Snell
Leon Stephens
Charlie Thomas
Theodore Thorn
John Tift
Ural L. Tift
Augustus Tillman
Leroy Tillman
Matthew Tillman
Ralph Tillman
Willie James Tillman
Ivory Toney
Robert Valentine
George Walker
Jacob Walker
Therman Walker
Richardson Western
Paul Weston
William White
Anderson Williams
Clarence Edward Williams
E.L. Williams
James Williams
Jerry Williams
Robert Williams II
Walter Ray Williams
Ralph Wimbish
Eddie Winston
Henry Woodard

A Historic Timeline

1528 Sailing with explorer Pánfilo de Narváez, freeborn Moroccan Esteban de Dorantes is possibly the first black man to visit the Florida sub-peninsula that would become Pinellas County.

1868 John Donaldson and Anna Germain, the woman who later became his wife, become the first people of color to settle permanently in the frontier community that would become St. Petersburg.

1888–1889 African American workers who helped build the Orange Belt Railway begin to move here, settling in an area labeled Pepper Town. It is just east of what became Ninth Street South, along what became Third and Fourth Avenues.

1890–1900 Another African American community begins to form along Ninth Street South, south of First Avenue South. It is called Cooper's Quarters, and was the beginning of what eventually became known as the Gas Plant area.

1894 The Bethel AME Church is founded at 912 Third Avenue North. An African American community known as Methodist Town grows around it.

1910 St. Petersburg's population is 4,127, including 1,098 African American residents—or about 27 percent—according to the federal census.

Davis Academy, later to become Davis Elementary, opens at 944 Third Avenue South, the first formal school for African Americans.

1913 The Democratic Party conducts a "whites only" primary in a city election. Another "unofficial" one would be held in 1921, and a 1930s city charter had provision for a white primary.

1914 At Ninth Street South and Second Avenue, townspeople and nightriders from the countryside lynch John Evans, an African American suspected of murdering white photographer Ed Sherman. The murdered white man's lawyer told his hometown Camden, New Jersey, newspaper that city leaders met in secret to plan the lynching.

1920 St. Petersburg's population is 14,237, including 2,444 African Americans—or about 17 percent—according to the federal census.

Adding weight to segregation policies, St. Petersburg police say they will arrest white men found at night in black areas of town, whatever their age or social standing.

1923 Mercy Hospital opens at 1344 Twenty-second Street South to serve African Americans.

1926 Jordan Elementary School, named for Elder Jordan Sr., opens on Ninth Avenue South just west of Twenty-second Street.

1927 Gibbs High School opens near Ninth Avenue South and Fargo Street, about a half mile west of Jordan Elementary. According to community lore, black students walked from Davis Academy at 944 Third Avenue South to stake claim to the new school, built for but never used by white elementary students. The school was named for Jonathan C. Gibbs, an African American who served as Florida's secretary of state and superintendent of public instruction during the Reconstruction era. The high school was in the middle of an undeveloped, wooded area jokingly referred to as "bear country."

1930 St. Petersburg's population is 40,425, including 7,416 African Americans—or about 18 percent—according to the federal census.

1931 A new city charter includes a clause banning white people from living or having a business in black neighborhoods, while forbidding black people from doing the same in white neighborhoods. It proved impractical to enforce.

1936 The city council approves a resolution to make all African Americans live west of Seventeenth Street and south of Sixth Avenue South. The southern boundary generally is considered to be Fifteenth Avenue South. Like the charter provision five years earlier that required business and residential segregation, the resolution couldn't be enforced to the letter.

1937 In full regalia, the Ku Klux Klan marches in July through black neighborhoods, including Twenty-second Street, to keep black voters away from a referendum.

In October, an African American man shoots two white police officers in Campbell Park. Officer James Thornton dies on the scene and Officer William Newberry dies a day later. Police canvass black neighborhoods, and white mobs terrorize black residents. Police catch J.O. "Honeybaby" Moses and shoot him dead. Whites try to steal the body. Some accounts say it was dragged down the street.

1938 Educator Noah Griffin is beaten by police at a teachers' picnic in Shore Acres in the northeast section of St. Petersburg, a white neighborhood. The city manager had given the educators verbal permission to the use the section, but the police were not aware of it.

1939 Construction begins on Jordan Park, the city's first housing project, a block west of Twenty-second Street just south of Ninth Avenue South. The first resident arrives on April 10, 1940.

The *St. Petersburg Times* begins publishing a "Negro news page" that appears only in black neighborhoods.

1940 St. Petersburg's population is 60,812, including 11,982 African Americans—or about 20 percent—according to the federal census.

1941 The second phase of Jordan Park is completed.

1944 U.S. Supreme Court rules that "whites only" primary elections are unconstitutional.

1946 Reflecting the opening of Jordan Park and the end of World War II, a record-high fifty-eight businesses are open on Twenty-second Street, including two drugstores and several grocery stores and restaurants.

1950 St. Petersburg's population is 96,738, including 13,977 African Americans—about 14 percent—according to the federal census.

1952 Sixteenth Street School opens at 701 Sixteenth Street South to serve African Americans in grades kindergarten through eight. It later is known as Sixteenth Street Junior High.

1954 U.S. Supreme Court strikes down school desegregation as unconstitutional. In St. Petersburg, Dr. Robert Swain Jr. breaks the Fifteenth Avenue South "red line," which defines where African Americans can live and open businesses. Swain, an oral surgeon, crosses the line by opening an office at 1501 Twenty-second Street South. At first the city refuses to issue building permits but relents when Swain threatens to sue.

1955 Rosa Parks refuses to give up her seat on a Montgomery, Alabama, bus. Her act launches a black passenger bus boycott and leads to a Supreme Court ruling that laws requiring segregation on buses are unconstitutional. In St. Petersburg, six African Americans sue to end segregation at St. Petersburg's downtown swimming spots. In 1957, the Supreme Court rules in favor of Fred Alsup, Ralph Wimbish, Willet Williams, Naomi Williams, Chester James Jr. and Harold Davis.

1956 Dr. Swain opens some apartments next to his office at 1501 Twenty-second Street South. They are built to accommodate black Major League baseball players, barred by segregation policies from staying in white-operated hotels during spring training.

1957 Congress passes Voting Rights Act.

1958 Despite the Supreme Court's decision the year before, the city refuses to integrate the downtown pool and beach, choosing to close them instead. The issue gradually dissolves as hoteliers and others dependent on the tourist industry worry that the closure will cost them money.

1958–1966 The Twenty-second Street South neighborhood hits its heyday, peaking in 1960, when there are 111 businesses open. The list includes doctors, lawyers, restaurants, bookkeeping and accounting services, groceries, pharmacies, pool halls and taverns, variety stores, service stations, shoe and clothing stores, a photo studio, furniture stores and a post office substation.

1960 St. Petersburg's population is 181,298, including 24,080 African Americans—or about 13 percent—according to the federal census.

Lunch counter sit-ins at such Central Avenue stores as Woolworth's, Liggett's, Rexall, McCrory's and Kress lead to the desegregation of most public dining places by 1961. Webb's City and Maas Brothers are among the downtown department stores picketed.

1961 Freedom Riders begin traveling throughout the South, challenging segregated interstate bus service. In St. Petersburg, the Citizens Cooperative Committee, consisting of several African American civil rights leaders, including Dr. Alsup, Dr. Wimbish and his wife C. Bette Wimbish and the Reverend Enoch Davis, took in the Freedom Riders during their visit here.

At Mound Park Hospital (now Bayfront Medical Center) Dr. Alsup admits the first black patient, though the hospital still is largely segregated.

Rosalie Peck, the former Rose Swain, and Frankie Howard are the first black students admitted to St. Petersburg Junior College.

1963 An estimated quarter-million civil rights supporters stage a march on Washington, D.C.; in St. Petersburg, three new, one-floor wings are added to Mercy Hospital, bringing bed capacity to seventy-eight.

1964 Congress enacts a sweeping Civil Rights Act banning segregation in hotels and restaurants and discrimination in employment; meanwhile, "Freedom Summer" sees massive African American voter registration efforts in Mississippi while extremists fight back with bombings and the murder of three rights workers. In St. Petersburg, more African American patients are being admitted to Mound Park, where admission has become a matter of physician-patient choice.

1965 Twelve African American police officers sue their employer, the City of St. Petersburg, for the right to patrol neighborhoods other than black ones, and for the right to arrest white citizens. The officers lost the first round in federal district court, but won on appeal.

1967 The *St. Petersburg Times* ends publication of the Negro news pages at the urging of African American staff member Peggy Peterman.

Davis Elementary School closes.

1968 The city's sanitation workers strike from May through August for better pay, working conditions and benefits. The strike leads to unrest, and in August, four nights of rioting occur. Several businesses are burned, including some white-owned stores on Twenty-second Street South.

The chamber of commerce forms the biracial Community Alliance to address problems in the wake of the sanitation strike. Membership initially included twenty-one white members and twelve black members. Black members included accountant David Welch, educator John Hopkins,

Manhattan Casino owner George Grogan, Dr. Gilbert Leggett and the Reverend McNeal Harris.

Frank W. Peterman Sr. becomes the first African American in the county to win a primary election for the state legislature. It was also about this time that Alvin Downing, a widely known musician who served with the famed Tuskegee Airmen, becomes the first African American to be named to the city housing authority.

1969 C. Bette Wimbish is the first African American elected to the city council.

1970 St. Petersburg's population is 216,232, including 31,911 African Americans—about 15 percent—according to the federal census.

Gibbs High School football players Robert Newton and Vincent Williams are killed by lightning as the team practiced on Labor Day. The Gibbs football field is named in their honor.

1971 Court-ordered busing desegregates Pinellas schools countywide. Pinellas is among the last counties in the state to integrate its schools but is the first Florida school district to use busing for integration. Some violence took place at Dixie Hollins and Boca Ciega high schools, but integration generally was accomplished peacefully.

1974–1981 Families and businesses are relocated and Interstate 275 is built through the Twenty-second Street neighborhood, changing the street's dynamic. Officials relocated residents from several neighborhoods, including the traditional African American communities.

1975 Jordan Elementary School closes

1980 St. Petersburg's population is 238,647, including 40,903 African Americans—about 17 percent—according to the federal census.

1981 David Welch, scion of a St. Petersburg pioneer family, is elected to the city council. Welch served two four-year terms, sat out an election, then was reelected to another four-year term in 1993.

1982 Doug Jamerson is elected to the state legislature. His election follows a successful campaign for single-member voting districts by lawyer Morris Milton and several others, including activists Watson Haynes and Perkins Shelton. Jamerson was appointed chairman of the Florida House of Representatives Housing Committee in 1988. One of the first three black students to attend Bishop Barry High School (later named St. Petersburg Catholic), Jamerson was appointed state education commissioner by Governor Lawton Chiles.

1984 The two huge cylinders known as the Gas Plant, which gave a neighborhood its name, are dismantled to make way for what would become Tropicana Field, home of Major League baseball's Tampa Bay Devil Rays. The neighborhood's housing, businesses and churches were soon to be swept away.

1987 After considerable debate, the city council renames Ninth Street Dr. Martin Luther King Jr. Street in honor of the slain civil rights leader.

1988 To build a parking lot for the Major League baseball stadium, the city acquires Laurel Park, a low-income housing complex. Two years later, the housing authority relocates 168 residents.

Bethel AME Church in Methodist Town becomes the first historic structure of significance to the black community to be named a local historic landmark.

1990 St. Petersburg's population is 238,629, including 46,726 African Americans—or about 20 percent—according to the federal census.

1993 The city earmarks $272,000 in federal grant money to encourage Twenty-second Street South redevelopment from Fifth to Twenty-second Avenues South.

1994 The city council designates the Manhattan Casino and Mercy Hospital sites as historic. It also approves a revitalization plan for the street, noting that vacant lots make up 25 percent of the street's land use.

1996 Two nights of racial disturbances occur in St. Petersburg, one in October and another in November, after police fatally shoot TyRon Lewis, an African American man. A liquor store at the intersection of Twenty-second Street and Eighteenth Avenue South is burned down.

1997 Goliath Davis, a son of Methodist Town, is named by Mayor David Fischer the first African American police chief. His tenure did much to improve relations between city hall and black neighborhoods.

Frank Peterman Jr. is elected to the St. Petersburg City Council. In 2000, thirty-two years after his father won a legislative primary race but lost in the general election, Peterman is elected to the Florida House of Representatives.

The city buys the old Mercy Hospital site. The city council also declares Dr. Robert Swain's dental office and adjacent apartments on Twenty-second Street and Fifteenth Avenue South to be historic sites.

1998 City officials say they plan to develop an industrial park on nineteen acres bordered by Twenty-second Street, Fifth Avenue South and Interstate 275. Later, a Job Corps center is planned for the site.

1999 Demolition begins at Jordan Park and many residents move elsewhere so work can start on Hope VI, the new public housing project being built on the same site.

2000 St. Petersburg's population is 248,232, including 55,502 African Americans—or about 22 percent—according to the federal census. Federal officials approve final plans for Hope VI.

2001 Goliath Davis is named deputy mayor by Mayor Rick Baker. He will spearhead Baker's initiative in Midtown, the name given to a section of the city containing many African American neighborhoods.

2002 Mary Brown becomes the first African American elected to the Pinellas County School Board.

The city buys the Manhattan Casino, which closed in 1968. An architect is hired to do a restoration plan. The last residents leave a Twenty-second Street neighborhood where work is starting on the industrial park's first stage.

2003 The Center for Achievement opens on Twenty-second Street and is designated the Midtown Campus of St. Petersburg College. It also offers other services, such as child care for people attending classes.

2004 The Johnnie Ruth Clarke Medical Center opens on the historic Mercy Hospital site, offering a number of services to neighborhood residents.

A renovated Boys and Girls Club opens in the old Royal Theater building.

2005 A new Sweetbay supermarket opens at Tangerine Plaza on Twenty-second Street South. It is the neighborhood's first such shopping center.

A Sampling of Businesses, 1937–1947

METHODIST TOWN

1. Northside Lunch Room Dine and Dance, 299 Jackson Street North, R.   Williams, proprietor.
2. McDonald's Grocery and Fresh Meat Market, Third Avenue and Eleventh Street North, L.W. McDonald, proprietor.
3. Streamlined Cut Rate Market Grocery, 1023 Burlington Avenue North.
4. Bill's Cafe, 299 Jackson Street North, Bill and Willie Gregory, proprietors.
5. Sophia's Beauty Shop, 1000 Burlington Avenue North.
6. Green Palace Café, 299 Jackson Street North.
7. Twilight Sandwich Shop, Burlington Avenue and Tenth Street North.
8. Bertha Lee's Beauty Shop, 241 Tenth Street North.
9. Cecil's Shoe Shine Parlor, 1023 Burlington Avenue North, Cecil Odom, proprietor.
10. Eloise's Beauty Shop, 1000 Burlington Avenue North, Eloise Johnson, proprietor.
11. Tenth Street Cafe, 245 Tenth Street North, Oscar Moore, proprietor.
12. Powell's Seafood and Grocery. 216 Jackson Street North.
13. George's Pool Room, Burlington Avenue and Jackson Street North, George "DeBose" Williams, proprietor.

THE GAS PLANT AREA

1. Ann's Hat Shop, 900 Third Avenue South, Ann Quinn, proprietor.
2. Public News Stand, 998 Second Avenue South, Verne E. Berry, proprietor.
3.   Kelly's Tailoring and Alterations, 984 Second Avenue South, Major Kelly, proprietor.
4.   Flossie's Bar-B-Q Stand, Sixteenth Street and Second Avenue South.
5.   LaVanity Beauty Shop, 929 Third Avenue South, Isabel Simmons, proprietor.
6. Modernistic Cleaners, E.L. Fountain, manager.

7. United Shoe Repair, 980 Second Avenue South, Professor W.L. Bradley, proprietor.

8. B.C. Logan's Cash Grocery, 1001 Third Avenue South, B.C. Logan, proprietor.

9. Elijah J. Jones, Tonsorial Expert, 940 Second Avenue South, E.J. Jones, proprietor.

10. Selena's Beauty Salon, 1576 Third Avenue South, Selena Fuller, proprietor.

11. Louise's Rainbow Beauty Shop, 1415 Third Avenue South.

12. Ritz Carlton Dining Room, 960 Second Avenue South.

13. Citizen's Lunch Room 948 Second Avenue South, Ted Williams, proprietor.

14. J.B. Smith's Grocery, 1220 Third Avenue South, J.B. Smith, proprietor.

15. Printing of All Kinds, 1026 Third Avenue South and 224 Fifteenth Street South.

16. Smitty's Tailor Shop, Dry Cleaning and Pressing, 996 Second Avenue South.

17. Nesbitt's Quick Lunch and Home Cooking, 206 Tenth Street South, Herman Nesbitt, proprietor.

18. Henderson's Service Station, 490 Sixteenth Street South, Jesse Henderson, proprietor.

19. Johnson's Cafe, 447 Fourteenth Street South.

20. Hick's Service Station, 436 Sixteenth Street South, Peter Hicks, proprietor.

21. B&B Cafe, 952 Second Avenue South.

22. Johnson's Shoe Shine Parlor, 960 Second Avenue South.

23. Brown's Shoe Service, 308 Eleventh Street South.

The Twenty-second Street South Community

1. Barnes Radio and TV Repair, Ninth Avenue South, Twenty-second Street South, Walter Barnes, proprietor.

2. Blankumsee's Grocery, 821 Twenty-fifth Street South.

3. Morgan's Grocery and Fish Market, Eighth Avenue and Twenty-second Street South.

4. G.W. Jones One-Stop Service Station, 1311 Twenty-second Street South, G.W. Jones, proprietor.

5. Flint's Grocery, 709 Twenty-second Street South, proprietor.

6. Kleckley's Barber Shop, 937 Twenty-second Street South, Oscar Kleckley, proprietor.

7. Ethel's Beauty Salon, 2139 Ninth Avenue South, Ethel Bludson, proprietor.

8. The Blue Rose Cafe, 901 Twenty-fourth Street South, L.E. Hughes, proprietor.

9. Dealma's Koppy Kat Beauty Shop, Dealma Fountain, proprietor.

This information is taken from Gibbs High School yearbooks.

Fun and Names

Nicknames suggest familiarity; a sense of closeness among friends, acquaintances, things, pets and places. The practice has been around for thousands of years. *Morris Dictionary of Word and Phrase Origins* says nicknames have been used since Anglo-Saxon times when surnames were unknown and nicknames were added to help identify the person. What still is amazing centuries later is how nicknames are born, take root, grow, supersede and replace proper names to the extent that pseudonyms are used exclusively in everyday conversations.

In St. Petersburg, as the city continues to grow and change in many ways, historic corridors are revived. Landmarks disappear. Once familiar streets, avenues, highways and byways are now host to new, attractive landscapes with explosions of blossoming faunas and floras. New buildings rise and new businesses appear. New housing and hope keep locals of long-standing residency speaking of neighborhoods now long gone. They disappeared with the indisputable renaissance that began in the late twentieth century and which spawned unprecedented change.

An interesting exception to all renaissance "newness" evident throughout the city is that nicknames of long gone historic black neighborhoods (specifically designed and tightly controlled to accommodate Jim Crow times) are still expressed among longtime residents in reference to the crowded neighborhoods of trying times that no longer exist.

Methodist Town alone maintained its original name. Throughout its long existence, it escaped the popular practice of nicknaming, probably due to the fact that it was named after Bethel AME Church, the oldest black church in St. Petersburg, founded on the north side of town by the Reverend J.S. Braswell in November 1894.

The neighborhood, with its close proximity to the church, maintained its identity as Methodist Town until it was demolished and renamed Jamestown for Chester James Sr., one of its early residents.

But few other areas were so spared. Neighborhoods with exotic nicknames—such as Pepper Town, Bolita Alley, Forty Quarters, the Gas Plant and Little Egypt, to name a few—were identified as such and to this day are so remembered.

Legal names were probably known only in terms of legal descriptions, city directories, slum landlords and a few savvy citizens.

Nicknames given to people, especially when they were young, also could last a lifetime.

Nostalgic, fun trips through any of the early Gibbs High School yearbooks are reminders that Eugene McCoy was "Jeep"; Henry Dandy was "Penny"; James Keys was "Security Vance"; Charles James was "Wham"; and James Thomas Lewis was "Little Buddy."

Alfred Ayer was "Gig"; Edward Fuller, "Jive"; Fred Grayson, "Wo-Wo"; Louis McCoy, "Chuck"; and Willie Woodard, "Skin."

Reasons for certain nicknames—like they were for neighborhoods—are sometimes obvious, such as Everett Wallace's "Old Faithful" moniker testifying to his loyalty, Robert Harris's "Party Rob" suggesting his good-time nature and Frank Grayson's "Pee Wee" indicative of his diminutive stature.

But sometimes nicknames' origins are obscure:

Cleveland Johnson was "Mole"; James McCoy was "Moody Goo"; Otto Fuller was "Ditto"; and Fleming Lane was "Chipmunk."

There was Althea Jones as "Tubby"; George Cooper as "Buster"; Leroy Barton, as "B.J."; and Charley Thomas as "Chilly Three."

Some old-timers will remember these:

Albert Brown, "Two-Four"; Lucious Sheely, "Pike"; Gus Lane, "Pee-Wee"; Theodore Hutchison, "Flair"; T.C. Stockton, "Top Cat"; Willie James, "Cool Breeze"; and Theodore Washington, "Snag."

There was Leroy Protho, called "Jay Bird"; Henry Woodard, "Fat Meat"; and Clarence Williams, "Shad."

A few more:

Theodore Gadson, "Hoddy Doddy"; Bernard Denson, "Pa Didley"; and "Shelly Belly," whose real name to this day escapes the memories of so many who knew him well. Frederick Douglas McCoy was "John Bull" and Freddie Gaskin is forever remembered as "Al Dumas."

Female students won nicknames as well:

Eunice Smith was "Lis"; Glorious McNeil was "Gem"; Eula Mae Sowell was "Shorty"; Helen Thompson was "Skipper."

Rosalie Peck, this book's coauthor, was known as "Red"; Willie Mae Harrington as "Meg"; Silver Lee Thompson as "Chubby"; Naomi Campbell as "Neci"; and Ernestine McGarrah as "Sister."

Otelia Plummer was called "T.T." by her friends; Ruby Walker was known as "Snookie"; Verna Mae Davis as "Pee-Wee"; Pauline Givens as "Pie"; and Rosanna Walker as "Pudding."

Lena May Francis was called "Nancy"; Mildred Johnson, "Peaches"; Elouise Gibson, "Gipp"; Lola Mae Washington, "Snooks"; and Rosa Lee Snell was "Miss McLin," so dubbed because of her dignity mirroring revered teacher O.B. McLin's impressive demeanor.

During those fun high school years, when much was wrong with the way things were, a time when childhood mischief was mild and scholastic achievement of black students was high, Gibbs students did not spare assigning nicknames to their teachers.

Theodore Johnson was "Moon"; Julius Bradley was "Goo"; William McLauren was "Skee Ball"; Marcellus Henderson was "Chaucer"; W.A. Armwood was "John Dillinger"; P.M. Sunday was "Mr. Sunday Afternoon"; Corinne Young was "Old Ironsides"; Florence Williams was "Mickey Mouse"; and Ernest Ponder was "Peanut."

To the students' knowledge, teachers never knew about nicknames assigned to them and enjoyed on a daily basis by fun-loving youngsters behind their backs.

But who is to say?

Historic Churches

In the years 1912 and 1951, the Polk City directories specifically listed churches—1951 was the last year African American residents, businesses and places of worship were identified as such in Polk City directories. Pastors were not listed for every church.

1912

Bethel Baptist, Third Avenue South and Tenth Street, C.H. Holley.

Christian Church, Fourth Avenue North and Twelfth Street.

Church of God, Second Avenue North and Williams Court, A.J. Simmons.

Mount Temor Baptist, Second Avenue South and Eighth Street.

Bethel AME, Third Avenue North and Williams Court.

Stewart's Chapel, Eighth Street South and Lincoln, S.L. Reece.

Mount Olive Primitive Baptist, 306 Williams Court, William Ford.

1951

Antioch Baptist, 1438 Second Avenue South.

Bethel Metropolitan Baptist, 301 Tenth Street South, George W. Jenkins.

First Baptist Institutional, Second Avenue South, Major J. Sherard.

First Mount Zion Baptist, 1120 Union Street.

Friendship Missionary Baptist, First Avenue South and Twenty-fourth Street, Johnnie L. Cooper.

Galilee Missionary Baptist, 1305 Elmore Avenue, Frank Cubby.

Macedonia Free Will Baptist, 2367 Seventh Avenue South.

Mount Carmel Missionary Baptist, 1111 Erie Street South, William Johnson.

Mount Olive Primitive Baptist, 310 Tenth Street North, Oliver B. Bartley.

Mount Zion Primitive Baptist, 2051 Ninth Avenue South, Robert Fraser.

Mount Zion Progressive Baptist, 1002 Twentieth Street South, Louis McCree.

Pleasant Grove Baptist, Ninth Avenue South and York Street.

Primitive Baptist, 809 Union Street.

Saint Antioch Baptist, 1438 Second Avenue South.

Saint Mark's Missionary Baptist, 344 Eleventh Street North, Willie J. Glover.

Saint Paul's Missionary Baptist, 245 Eleventh Street North, Charles H. Gardner.

Second Bethel Baptist, 506 Sixteenth Street South, Enoch D. Davis.

Travelers Rest Missionary Baptist, 1600 Fifth Avenue South, Leoza A. Latimore.

Saint Augustine Episcopal, 1625 Sixth Avenue South.

Bethel AME, Third Avenue North and Tenth Street, A.P. Postell.

McCabe Memorial Methodist, 357 Ninth Street South, Anderson C. Trice.

Moore's Chapel AME, 3041 Fairfield Avenue South, Benjamin T. Ross.

Stewart Memorial Methodist, 2163 Ninth Avenue South, S.L. Reece.

Trinity Presbyterian, Ninth Avenue South and Nineteenth Street, Oscar M. McAdams.

Church of Christ, 814 Twentieth Street South, Samuel J. Dudley.

Church of Christ, 2427 Irving Avenue South.

Church of God, 915 Second Avenue North.

Church of God in Christ, 1400 Ninth Avenue South, Thomas Wheeler.

Church of the Living God, 235 Tenth Street North.

Church of the Living God, 1908 Fairfield Avenue South.

Elim Seventh Day Adventist, 2147 Ninth Avenue South.

Fire Baptized Holiness Church of God, 2515 Harrington Avenue South.

Jehovah's Witnesses Kingdom Hall, 402 Twelfth Street South.

Queen Street Church of God, 731 Queen Street South.

Sanctified Church of God, 2410 Harrington Avenue South.

Triumphant Holiness Church, 1828 Carolina Court South, Joseph C. Johnson.

This information was taken from Polk City directories.

Notes

Chapter 1: The Old Ties

1. Claudette Renney Dean, "The Moon Shed a Tear," typescript, n.d.
2. James King, interview by Jon Wilson, January 15, 2007.
3. Jon Wilson, "Masonic Lodge Was First Site for Library," *St. Petersburg Times*, November 26, 2003, Neighborhood Times section.
4. The development and disappearance of this community can be charted with Polk City directories, 1925–1956.
5. Paul Barco, interview by Jon Wilson, November 11, 1981.
6. Raymond O. Arsenault, *St. Petersburg and the Florida Dream* (Norfolk/Virginia Beach, VA: The Donning Co., 1988), 265.

Chapter 2: Remember the Gladiators

7. Jon Wilson, "A Team Plays into History," *St. Petersburg Times*, July 19, 2006, Neighborhood Times section. The article described the events as they appear in this book.
8. Evelyn Newman Phillips, "An Ethnohistorical Analysis of the Political Economy among African Americans in St. Petersburg, Florida," PhD diss., University of South Florida, 1994. Available online at the Olive B. McLin Community History Project, University of South Florida, http://www.nelson.usf.edu/mclin/res.1.html
9. Ibid.
10. Ibid.
11. King, interview.
12. Horace Nero, interview by Jon Wilson, December 11, 2006.

Chapter 3: Home in the Neighborhoods

13. Elijah Gosier, "'20s Beach Boom Banished Blacks," *St. Petersburg Times*, February 12, 1990, City Times section.
14. Phillips, "An Ethnohistorical Analysis."
15. King, interview.
16. "City Hall Flags Lowered," *St. Petersburg Times*, March 8, 1958, B section.
17. Gwendolyn Reese, interview by Rosalie Peck, December 4, 2006.
18. Mordecai Walker, interview by Rosalie Peck, March 22, 2007.
19. St. Petersburg City Report, "Methodist Town," n.d, Carter G. Woodson Museum of African American History, St. Petersburg.
20. Arsenault, *St. Petersburg*, 126.
21. Mittie Walton Pounds, interview by Rosalie Peck, February 24, 2007.
22. Willie Lee Gregory, interview by Rosalie Peck, December 2, 2006.
23. Goliath Davis III, interview by Rosalie Peck and Jon Wilson, April 9, 2006.
24. Scott Taylor Hartzell, "Activist Helped Salvage the Ghettoes, Win Rights," *St. Petersburg Times*, February 28, 2001, Neighborhood Times section.
25. Tim Phelps, "The James of Jamestown Faces Loss of Home There," *St. Petersburg Times*, May 20, 1975, B section.

Chapter 4: The Business of Life

26. Maria Vesperi, *City of Green Benches: Growing Old in a New Downtown* (Ithaca, NY: Cornell University Press, 1985), 36.
27. Dean, "The Moon."
28. Clarence Welch, David Welch and Johnny Welch, interviews by Jon Wilson, September 17, 2007.
29. Craig Basse, "Flagmon Welch, 87, Owner of Firewood Yard," *St. Petersburg Times*, June 27, 1989, B section.
30. Gregory, interview.
31. Scott Taylor Hartzell, "By His Own Bootstraps, A Cobbler Prospered," *St. Petersburg Times*, November 20, 2002, Neighborhood Times section.
32. Phillips, "An Ethnohistorical Analysis."
33. James Harper, "Around the Dome, Echoes of the Past," *St. Petersburg Times*, March 29, 1998, B section.
34. Frances N. Pinckney, "Owner/Operator of Tavern-Café Over Four-Decades," Grayson Family Archive. Available online at the Olive B. McLin Community History Project, University of South Florida, http://www.nelson.usf.edu/mclin/grayarticle1.html

35. "Black Publisher Dies At &3," *Weekly Challenger*, August 2, 2001, front section.
36. "Deaths Elsewhere," *Honolulu Star-Bulletin*, August 2, 2001, Obituary section.
37. Phillips, "An Ethnohistorical Analysis."

CHAPTER 5: BATTLING JIM CROW'S TERRORISTS

38. Walter Fuller, *St. Petersburg and its People* (St. Petersburg, FL: Great Outdoors Publishing Co., 1972), 282.
39. Phillips, "An Ethnohistorical Analysis."
40. Lula Grant, interview by Jon Wilson, December 2, 1981.
41. Fuller, *St. Petersburg*, 281.
42. Luther Atkins, interview by Jon Wilson, November 10, 1081.
43. Robert L. Zangrando, *The NAACP Crusade Against Lynching, 1909–1950* (Philadelphia: Temple University Press, 1980), 3.
44. The *St. Petersburg Times* and the *St. Petersburg Independent* reported these details on November 11, 1914, and November 12, 1914, respectively. Much of this account was gleaned from old newspaper files.
45. The *St. Petersburg Times* published accounts containing these details on November 12. Microfilm of the edition shows a section of the front page ripped out where photographs would have been placed. In the 1981 interview, resident Luther Atkins said the newspaper published photos of the black men suspected.
46. Atkins, interview.
47. Ralph Reed, interview by Jon Wilson, December 5, 1981.
48. Stanley Sweet, interview by Jon Wilson, January 18, 1982.
49. *St. Petersburg Times*, November 12, 1914.
50. *Camden Courier*, November 20, 1914.
51. Minutes of the Circuit Court, Microfilm No. 1, Book No. 1, 128, Pinellas County Courthouse, Clearwater, Florida; *Tampa Tribune*, September 22, October 19, 22, 23, 1915; *St. Petersburg Independent*, October 22, 1915; *St. Petersburg Times*, October 23, 1915.

CHAPTER 6: HELPING BUILD A COMMUNITY

52. Jon Wilson, "Pioneering Policemen," *St. Petersburg Times*, March 25, 2007, Neighborhood Times section. Much of the account of the police officers' suit against the St. Petersburg city government is taken from this article.
53. Phillips, "An Ethnohistorical Analysis."

54. Jon Wilson, "Rosa Jackson's Tradition Continues," *St. Petersburg Times*, November 19, 1997, Neighborhood Times section.
55. Laura Lee, "Thomas Jackson,"*St. Petersburg Times*, February 11, 2004, C section.

Chapter 7: The Power of the Word

56. Enoch Douglas Davis, *On the Bethel Trail* (St. Petersburg, FL: Valkyrie Press, 1979), 21–22.
57. The Negro news pages were published by the *St. Petersburg Times* between 1939 and 1967. They were inserted for delivery in black neighborhoods only.
58. Jon Wilson, "Nursery Named Historic Property," *St. Petersburg Times*, August 16, 1998, Neighborhood Times section.
59. Phillips, "An Ethnohistorical Analysis."
60. City of St. Petersburg, "Local Historic Landmarks," Urban Design and Historic Preservation Division, http://www.stpete.org/BethelAME.htm
61. Rosemary J. Brown, *St. Petersburg's Historic Suite* (St. Petersburg, FL: St. Petersburg Arts Commission, 1980), 16.
62. Elaine Jenkins, interview by Rosalie Peck, October 8, 2007.
63. Karen Loeb, *St. Petersburg's Historic Suite* (St. Petersburg, FL: St. Petersburg Arts Commission, 1980), 30.
64. Davis, *Bethel Trail*, 42.
65. Ibid, 67.

Chapter 8: How Much Remains?

66. Harper, "Around the Dome."
67. Ibid.
68. Waveney Ann Moore, "Black Leadership Changes with Times," *St. Petersburg Times*, May 18, 2003, Neighborhood Times section.
69. Betty Hayward, "She Volunteers a Rich, Full Voice," *St. Petersburg Times*, November 29, 1994, special section.
70. Jon Wilson, "Beloved 'Mama Mattie' Gardner is Dead at 103," *St. Petersburg Times*, December 4, 2005, Neighborhood Times section.
71. Jon Wilson, "Banquet Will Honor Educator," *St. Petersburg Times*, May 16, 2007, Neighborhood Times section.

About the Authors

Jon Wilson is a lifelong journalist, having been a reporter, editor and editorial writer at the St. Petersburg Times during his thirty-five-year career there. He has a master's degree in journalism and has been pursuing a master of liberal arts with a focus on Florida studies.

Rosalie Peck is a retired social worker with a master's in the field. After graduating from Bethune-Cookman College, she worked in Detroit and Los Angeles before returning to St. Petersburg in the 1970s. She retired in 1978 and now devotes most of her time to writing. In 1992, she was named Ms. Senior Florida. She is currently the executive editor of the Weekly Challenger.

Jon and Rosalie teamed up to write St. Petersburg's Historic 22nd Street South, published by The History Press in 2006.

Visit us at
www.historypress.net